STILETTO NETWORK

STILETTO NETWORK

INSIDE THE WOMEN'S POWER CIRCLES THAT ARE CHANGING THE FACE OF BUSINESS

PAMELA RYCKMAN

AMACOM AMERICAN MANAGEMENT ASSOCIATION

NEW YORK · ATLANTA · BRUSSELS · CHICAGO · MEXICO CITY
SAN FRANCISCO · SHANGHAI · TOKYO · TORONTO · WASHINGTON, D.C.

Bulk discounts available. For details visit:
www.amacombooks.org/go/specialsales
Or contact special sales:
Phone: 800-250-5308 / E-mail: specialsls@amanet.org
View all AMACOM titles at: www.amacombooks.org
American Management Association: www.amanet.org

This publication is designed to provide accurate and authoritative information in regard to the subject matter covered. It is sold with the understanding that the publisher is not engaged in rendering legal, accounting, or other professional service. If legal advice or other expert assistance is required, the services of a competent professional person should be sought.

Library of Congress Cataloging-in-Publication Data

Ryckman, Pamela.
Stiletto network : inside the women's power circles that are changing the face of business / Pamela Ryckman.
    pages cm
Includes index.
ISBN-13: 978-0-8144-3253-2 (hardcover)
ISBN-10: 0-8144-3253-0 (hardcover)
1. Businesswomen. 2. Women executives. 3. Women in the professions. 4. Business networks. 5. Strategic alliances. I. Title.
HD6053.R93 2013
331.4'81658—dc23

                                                                2012051563

About AMA

American Management Association (www.amanet.org) is a world leader in talent development, advancing the skills of individuals to drive business success. Our mission is to support the goals of individuals and organizations through a complete range of products and services, including classroom and virtual seminars, webcasts, webinars, podcasts, conferences, corporate and government solutions, business books, and research. AMA's approach to improving performance combines experiential learning—learning through doing—with opportunities for ongoing professional growth at every step of one's career journey.

Printing number
10 9 8 7 6 5 4 3 2 1

This book about girls is dedicated to my boys.
To Bill, Will, George, and James for your
love, patience, and support.

CONTENTS

ACKNOWLEDGMENTS

Stiletto Network is a testament to the power of its thesis: that these networks work. This book was truly a collaborative effort, with incredible women across the globe opening doors, providing advice and guidance, and stepping in to help each time I got stuck. I will be forever grateful for both the opportunities they gave me and the faith they showed in me.

I owe a particular debt of gratitude to Susan Stautberg and Edie Weiner—two formidable, kind, brilliant, beautiful women who opened their "community of trust" to me. You are true role models, and it has been a profound joy to learn from you.

As I was writing *Stiletto Network*, I was devouring *Selected Quotations That Inspire Us to Think Bigger, Live Better, and Laugh Harder*, a gem of a compilation by Susan Stautberg and Theresa Berhendt. Many quotes seemed apt as I crafted my story, but one stuck with me. Oftentimes, when I'd relay my ideas to skeptical listeners (who inevitably countered with tales of bitchy bosses), I found myself quoting Susan quoting Daniel L. Reardon: "In the long run the pessimist may be proved right, but the optimist has a better time on the trip."

I fully believe *Stiletto Network* represents a new truth for women in the workplace, and it's an optimist's story—not to mention a hell of a lot of fun!

A special thank-you to Jillian Manus, who was a source (introduced by another source) before she became my super-agent who never gave up. She lives and breathes the inspiring message of this book. And I want to thank the team at AMACOM—Ellen Kadin, Barry Richardson, Andy Ambraziejus, Jenny Wesselmann, Irene Majuk, Rosemary Carlough, Cathleen Ouderkirk, and Erika Spelman.

I would also like to thank all the women who shared their stories with me. Thank you for welcoming me into your homes and friendships, and for trusting me with the intimate details of your lives.

This journey began with an invitation to the first "Alley to the Valley" conference in November 2010. The summer before, I started talking to Deborah Perry Piscione, an entrepreneur, and Janet Hanson, the founder of 85 Broads, who together organized this event. As high-powered women agreed to participate, Deborah and Janet asked if they'd be willing to speak with me for an article I was writing on "Alley to the Valley" for the *New York Times*. These ladies were the first to let me in, and this was when I first sensed that something exciting was happening in the world. Thank you, Deborah and Janet, for providing the spark.

I would be nowhere without my dream-team of readers, each of whom perused early drafts and provided comments and insight that shaped the book. First, to Allison Fabian Derfner, the closest thing I have to a college roommate as an adult. How lucky am I that my wonderful neighbor, the one I hang out with in pajamas as our boys wrestle in the hall, happens to have been the long-term Features Editor at *Harper's Bazaar*? Fate smiled on me when you moved in. May you forgive my incessant questions, and celebrate the end of pages slipped under your door. And to Megan Mulligan, my former editor at the *New York Sun*, and Lauren Foster, my former editor at the *Financial Times*. I am so fortunate to know you both as exceptional colleagues and dear friends.

Just when I didn't think I could feel more blessed, another set of advisers and advocates emerged when this book went into production. The PR dynamo Suzy Ginsburg rolled up her sleeves, even when I didn't have the budget to pay her—just because she believed in the story. Alexej Steinhardt and Elana Carroll of Round Hex went above and beyond for my website and graphics. Mary Beth O'Connor and Sheila Klehm offered counsel and so generously organized lunches with key influencers to help spread ideas, even before we'd met in person. Claudia Batten arrived with passion and spectacular expertise in brand-building and digital media (and fabulous shoes), and she pushed me to always think bigger. "Let's create a movement!" she said, and then mobilized her troops.

I have been overwhelmed by all of their kindness and enthusiasm, and in awe of their great big brains.

Finally, I want to thank my sons for being their sweet, curious, engaging, fun-loving selves; for teaching me to embrace the chaos; and for being almost as excited about this book as I am. And my parents, George and Janet Balbach, who said of course I could be the fastest runner in fourth grade. And my sister, Lauren Loutit, who keeps me sane. And Jennifer Wray, whose devotion to my children and help at home gives me the freedom to write. And most of all, my husband, Bill, without whose love and support none of this would be possible.

STILETTO NETWORK

INTRODUCTION

Who knew Nora Ephron was such a Harpy? Barbara Walters, that's who.

Following Ephron's death in June 2012, the *New York Post* reported that she and Walters were members of the Harpies, described as "a close-knit cadre of lunching ladies who've met to eat and argue over twelve years at Michael's, the Four Seasons, and '21.'"

The Harpies include other media moguls too, and according to my favorite tabloid, the ladies often gossip about Hillary—her whereabouts, her fatigue, her hair—and engage in "intense debate" over the latest headlines. "God forbid you were wrong," a Harpy insider told the *Post*, "or you were dismissed and reduced to rubble . . . with great affection." It seemed that these women were exacting and precise, that they held themselves and each other to high standards, and that they pushed and challenged their friends. But they did it with humor and ultimate kindness.

I was approaching my book deadline when I read about the Harpies at the breakfast table. "See?" I jumped up and cheered. "All the girls are doing it! It's sweeping the nation!"

As a cabal of bold-faced names, the Harpies are pretty swank in their own right. They're movers and shakers, no doubt. But, I wondered aloud, do they know they're part of something bigger? Do they know that their group and others just like it are changing the world?

My three sons rolled their eyes. They raced out the door to their all-boys school.

I didn't plan to write a book at this very moment in my life, but it's my family's consensus that with all the testosterone at home, I needed to talk to some girls. And once I started interviewing dynamic, motivated women, I found I couldn't stop. I didn't know exactly what was happening, but I knew it was important.

At the beginning, it was a gut feeling, a notion that I had unearthed something meaningful that was shaping women's lives. But I didn't yet realize how important it would be for me personally. I didn't know I'd end up living this story as I was writing it, that it would be the story that changed my life. But more on that later.

It all started at a women's conference in California. There, I met one female senior executive who introduced me to another and then another, and each one was fascinating and charismatic, engaging and kind, vulnerable and bold. They didn't carp about "balance" or lament not "having it all." They didn't feel oppressed and under siege, and their days weren't some dismal, tough slog. They took evident joy in both work and personal life, adoring jobs and families alike. "Why don't we ever see anything about women having fun at work?" one woman asked. "Sure, there are battles, but I work so hard and I love it. Can't we ever accentuate the joys over the battles?"

They didn't carp about "balance" or lament not "having it all." They took evident joy in both work and personal life, adoring jobs and families alike.

While it's not PC to say this, these ladies were also cute. I liked their outfits. They had chic shoes and healthy hair. Here were women comfortable in their own skin, not trying to dress and act and sound like guys. Here were the opposite of hoary archetypes—those sharp-elbowed, steamrolling, ball-busting bitches. And here was an antidote to the dreary navel-gazing and hairy-legged petulance of Women's Studies 101. These chicks were successful, but still really fun.

So what was their secret? I started listening and learning, observing how they made it all work. And before long, they were gushing about their girlfriends.

Professional women from their twenties to their seventies started recounting hilarious stories, and often they'd begin like this: "Well, in my dinner group. . . ." "Your dinner group?" I'd ask. "Who's in your dinner group? What do you do when you get together?" Eat, naturally. Drink, copiously. And gossip, naughtily. It all sounded like a blast.

I started to discover dinner groups and salons and coworking and networking circles in major cities across the United States. In almost every case, the women thought they were alone in assembling clusters of dear, smart girlfriends who met regularly to learn and share. They'd never heard of the other groups, and when I told them they were thrilled. "You're onto something," they'd say, and then introduce me to their pals.

At that point, I didn't have a thesis or a commissioned article or a book contract. All I had was a hunch. Yet accomplished, in-demand women agreed to talk to me. They made themselves available for open-ended interviews that, for all they knew, might go nowhere—just because a friend had asked them to. So many times in the course of reporting, I heard, "I never talk to the press. I'm only talking to you because so-and-so said to." The ladies were busy, but not too busy to do a favor for a friend.

I was captivated by their clandestine coteries, as I was trying to navigate my own professional life. Nine years ago, after my first son was born, I'd left a career in consulting and investment banking to become a journalist. I went to grad school, got pregnant again, took a hiatus, started freelancing, finished grad school, got pregnant again. Now I write from home while caring for young children. I work incredibly hard for a tiny fraction of the money I made before, but I'm around for my kids and I love my job.

The more conversations I had with women, the more I reflected on my own path. When I began trying to freelance, I was clawing my way into a new industry, working in a vacuum with no network of journalists or editors to guide me. I perused mastheads and targeted senior staff at dozens of publications. I researched and pitched and researched and pitched. Inevitably, I was met with silence. Editors didn't read my e-mails, much less return my calls.

I knew my previous experience was relevant—that I'd learned to interview, think logically, solve complex problems, and communicate—but editors didn't seem to agree. Did I need to take an entry-level job to prove myself? I'd worked twelve- to fifteen-hour days at an investment bank until three days before giving birth. I'd teamed up with great minds on challenging, stimulating projects and supported myself. Now, at any writing job I considered, I'd be earning less than I paid a nanny. I felt humbled and demoralized and irrelevant.

But writing had been my first love. And I knew I could be good at this, if someone would only give me a shot. Finally, someone did, when a prominent female writer put herself on the line. "Tell her I sent you," she said, directing me to an editor at the *New York Sun*. "Use my name."

As I spoke with vibrant ladies for this book and watched them lobby for one another, I realized that every opportunity I'd gotten in journalism had come through a woman: at the *New York Sun* (where I was the oldest living knocked-up intern, waddling in two afternoons per week—"Fatty will work for free!"), the *Financial Times*, and the *New York Times*. I've written for amazing male editors, but it was always a woman who got me through the door.

Why was that? Were women somehow more open to seeing that I, an untraditional candidate—sometimes pregnant, sometimes nursing, often wearing yoga pants (though obviously not to meetings)—had something worthy to offer? Did they, with their own struggles and juggles, somehow understand mine? Did it matter less to them how my work got done—sometimes taking calls from my bathroom, barricaded behind two sets of closed doors that rattled when my toddler crashed his Big Wheel in the hall—as long as it was on time and good quality?

I was doubly meticulous, and not just because I enjoyed the work, but because I feared no one would take me seriously. Years into my writing career, I was making progress, but I still wasn't where I wanted to be. I didn't feel particularly successful. But, I reassured myself, there would be time for that. If I'd focused on landing more and bigger scoops, that would have meant time away from my boys, time I could never recapture. To be the kind of mom I wanted to be, I felt I had to choose. My goals and dreams would wait.

And then something changed. Before I could acknowledge what was happening, women were helping me. I started landing interviews with powerful female sources because their friends had urged them to talk. Even before I asked, these women offered. "You ask good questions," they'd say. "You get what we do." Maybe my prior training was handy after all. "You need to talk to this person," they'd say, and immediately connect us by e-mail. "Here's her cell phone number," they'd say, and trust me with personal information for executives normally ensconced behind gatekeepers and a fortress of PR. "Tell her I sent you," they'd say. "Use my name."

I did, and doors flew open. Prominent women took my calls. "How can I help?" they asked, and answered my questions. They didn't qualify or censor themselves, and they didn't say everything was off the record. Because I'd come through a trusted friend, they just talked. They batted around ideas, and they told me about their work and dinner groups. They opened up about their families and their fears.

These women were so honest with me, and still I lied, a little. I didn't mention that I work from home, and I hid the fact that I'm often with my kids during the day and write late into the night. I worried that truly hard-core, accomplished women—the ones who sat in corner offices and business class—would write me off. I worried that they'd think I was weak for having compromised, that they would dismiss my choices.

But these women let me in, and every time I tripped and fretted, someone picked me up. At one point, I embarrassed myself and started crying at lunch with a sixty-year-old CEO who's become a great friend and mentor. I told her I'd stopped sleeping, that I was exhausted and scared and stressed, that I didn't feel good enough, and that I wasn't spending enough time with my kids. I felt like I was failing at everything and I was questioning all my choices.

"What if I've been wasting everyone's time? What if I just . . . suck?" I said, head in my hands. "Maybe I should do yoga."

"Fuck yoga," she laughed, waving her hand. But then she looked at me, stern and serious and straight in the eye. "You're doing edge work. You're creating and uncovering things. You're putting things together in a way no one else has. Whatever happens, you'll be fine. Just keep going." No one had ever said something like that to me, and as far as I knew, no one had ever thought it. I was having trouble believing in myself, but she believed in me. So of course I kept going.

> Stiletto Networks aren't about titles, and you don't need power or wealth to create one. Stiletto Networks are about trying to make your own personal dent in the world.

This is what Stiletto Networks have been doing for each other, and now it's what they've done for me. They've enabled me to take this next step in my career, to write my first book, to find a way to make my dreams happen now, even when I didn't think I was ready. They've inspired me, absorbed my weakness, and made me stronger.

What I've learned is that Stiletto Networks aren't about titles, and you don't need power or wealth to create one. Stiletto Networks are about trying to make your own personal dent in the world. For me that means writing books, while for others it means leading companies, directing schools, or rallying behind candidates. As my friend Claudia Batten, a serial entrepreneur, says, Stiletto Networks are about becoming "the biggest, boldest, bravest version of yourself that you can be."

This book is about groups that make women big, bold, and brave: the "Harpies" and "Power Bitches," "Babes in Boyland" and "Chicks in Charge." It's about what happens when bright, caring women—from their twenties to their seventies—come together to celebrate and unwind, debate and compare notes. But it's also about what happens when they leave the table, when the talking stops and the action starts. It's about how they mine their collective intelligence to realize their dreams or champion a cause, how they lift up their friends and push them forward, how they collaborate to ensure each woman gets what she needs—be it information, an introduction, a recommendation, a partnership, or a landmark deal. It's about women banding together to achieve their destinies and change the world.

Yet it's even more than that. When they talk about their clusters, women now use words like *life-changing. Destined. Fated. Magical. Meant to be.* These are terms unheard in business, words reserved for love. At first it's disconcerting, like walking in on your parents having sex, or overhearing your boss purr intimacies to his wife, or mistress. They're just not supposed to behave like that. Executive women aren't meant to act like girls, much less talk like Oprah.

But see it twice, three times, ten or twenty times over, and know the workplace will never be the same. Yes, these ladies have big jobs. They move real money. And still, so many influential women attribute recent victories to doing what comes naturally: listening to and advocating for treasured friends.

So this is a love story disguised as a business story, a tale of female friendship. It's a story of women whose huge hearts match their mighty brains. Women who choose passion over balance. Women who leap into life.

It's about the kind of woman so many of us are striving to be. And with help from our Stiletto Networks, we can.

A FORCE TO BE RECKONED WITH

Kim Moses never thought women would transform her life. She was already a force in blockbuster TV, producing and directing shows that won six Emmys and two Golden Globes. And she'd spent her early career in sports, after following her high school sweetheart—a football prodigy named Joe Montana—to Notre Dame. Now she had a loving husband and business partner, plus two teenage sons. Needless to say, Moses was accustomed to being the only woman in the room.

"Girl power" sounded lovely if chimerical, the province of utopian theorists. Women who'd spent enough time in the workforce knew better than to pine for some refuge of feminine support. It just wasn't part of Moses's reality—until she found herself at the center of The Vault.

The Vault isn't some secret society. It has no charter or clubhouse or rules. It's just a bunch of ladies gathering for dinner, at each other's homes, no less. But these gals happen to be tops in their fields, and in 2009, Moses had an urge to bring them together.

As cofounder of Sander/Moses Productions and Slam, a digital media company, Moses knew that go-getting women existed in C-suites and conference rooms, on mastheads and boards of directors. Yet they were tucked away in offices or zipping around on planes, and after work they ran home to care for their families. They weren't being seen, or seeing much of each other. So Moses called her friend Willow Bay, a television correspondent and *Huffington Post* editor, to suggest they assemble some busy women for a meal.

> *Large conferences didn't breed intimacy, but dinner at one another's houses just might.*

Moses and Bay had been to hundreds of formal networking events, and they grasped the importance of a filter. Large conferences didn't breed intimacy, but dinner at one another's houses just might. They wanted their group to be personal, not just business, and they hoped women would open up and forge friendships among equals. They contacted some women they knew and others they'd never met, targeting experts across a variety of industries, gals sure to possess an array of strategies and viewpoints. "I wanted to connect with women who had climbed and discovered and figured it out, instead of inheriting something. It's a different journey," Moses says. "I wanted to meet women who could tell their stories."

And Moses had a rags-to-riches tale of her own.

Life Was Not a Spectator Sport

Finding women she could relate to was especially important for Moses because she'd succeeded without ever having role models. She was raised in a poor coal-mining town in southwest Pennsylvania, a town with "good souls" but few options. There were three ways a woman could go: nurse, teacher, or wife. Men were athletes, or they ended up on welfare or in jail. Nobody went to college. "There was nothing to aspire to and no one to show you the way," she says. "My brothers and I were the few who went out into the world and didn't go back there."

Moses left home at age 19 to marry Montana and move to Indiana, where she worked in the Sports Information Office at Notre Dame while her husband began his rise toward the Hall of Fame. She loved live sports, but when the pair separated during Montana's senior year, Moses was abruptly shown the door. "We were a high-profile couple. They'd won the national championship, and Notre Dame made it clear they wanted me to move on. It was awkward for them," she says. "I was very hurt because I had worked hard and really felt I stood on my own. There were no women there and I had no one to turn to."

Moses followed a Notre Dame friend to Washington, D.C., where she labored in the trenches on Capitol Hill. There she saw at least a few women with power, women with ideas and opinions who, instead of just cheerleading from the sidelines, worked together with men toward common goals. She began putting herself through Georgetown, and she used her wits and gumption to score a spot with Al Gore supporting his efforts to halt climate change, but Moses saw that without a law degree, her Washington career would be limited. Plus, she wanted to follow her passion, and that meant sticking to sports.

Through family members and former colleagues at Notre Dame, Moses secured connections to ABC Sports and the NFL. She pursued projects when Congress went on hiatus several times a year, working on production teams at both college and professional levels, covering everything from bowling to basketball, not to mention nine Super Bowls and the 1984 Olympics.

It was the 1980s, the Reagan administration, and determined career girls were just starting to appear in the media, if as sexless, strident caricatures brandishing their *noms de guerre.* Sigourney Weaver sparred with Melanie Griffith in *Working Girl,* while in *Baby Boom,* Diane Keaton's "Tiger Lady" struggled to manage her ambition and an adopted daughter. All wore Reeboks over nude hose, shoulder pads over thick skin. Life, they were told, was not a spectator sport.

Even so, Moses worked with all men. Few arenas were more male-dominated than government and athletics, and often it felt like she'd left one locker room for another. "The Hill and then ABC and NBC Sports, it was a wild, rowdy group of guys. When you're in a man's world, it's really loud, noisy, and aggressive. I hadn't seen any women I wanted to be, whose job I wanted to have," she says. "Trying to find your voice is hard if you haven't seen someone else do it."

But Moses had drive and talent. She knew she could be successful, even in sports, if only someone would give her a chance. She started sending letters to sports producers in New York and Los Angeles. Finally, she received an offer from a Notre Dame graduate who worked for Don Ohlmeyer, a producer who'd expanded to mainstream entertainment and was now running his own shop. She ditched Georgetown and D.C. to join him.

Moses traveled frequently with Ohlmeyer Productions, and when she returned from one month-long trip to Florida for a Disney special, she found a new producer—Ian Sander—sitting across the hall. Sander was working with Ohlmeyer on a movie, and he and Moses became fast friends. They began dating three months later, once he'd left the firm, and about eight months into their romance, Moses brought him *Stolen Babies*.

Stolen Babies, a 1993 primetime drama on Lifetime television, starred Mary Tyler Moore, who won an Emmy for her performance. The film marked the beginning of a personal and professional collaboration for Sander and Moses that has lasted twenty years and garnered countless awards. The couple is now married, and together they own a production company known for its use of cutting-edge technology. In the mid-1990s, they produced *Profiler*, the first show to leverage the Internet to cultivate fans, and when it came time for their most recent hit, *Ghost Whisperer*—the CBS drama starring Jennifer Love Hewitt—they took everything they'd learned about digital platforms and started generating buzz well before the program aired. They organized events and fashioned an online crystal ball game, a graphic novel, video games, and a Web series from a ghost's point of view. Or, as Moses says, they created a 360-degree "total engagement experience" to nurture a base of devoted female followers.

Their marketing blitz worked. *Ghost Whisperer* averaged 10 million viewers its first season, more than any other Friday night show in 2005, and ran for five years. But for Moses, the fact that her show was built around a strong woman was as important as its overall success. "We were poised to have staying power, and we were the number one most talked about show online," she says. "We built *Ghost Whisperer* into a powerful brand with a woman at the core. I learned I was able to drive ratings with a predominantly female audience and build a loyal fan base and a powerhouse brand, all around a female role model."

Realizing the strength of her female brand set Moses thinking. She'd left the sausage-fest of sports and politics, and still she was surrounded by guys. She recalled a time years before, when she'd found herself sitting across from a bigwig at CBS, interviewing for a job she knew she could nail. She'd expressed her love of producing, revealed her background and need to support herself, and then she was floored by this man's hidebound response. "He said, 'You will never, ever work for a network because you don't have a college education,'" Moses says, still smarting. "The idea that this guy could step on my dream made me go after it more aggressively."

Now she was a big-time producer for the most prestigious networks, and she knew her shows were making an impact. So, she wondered, how is it possible—when women are the dominant viewers of network TV—that there aren't more female decision makers in the field?

"Even in Hollywood I didn't have a true infrastructure of women who understood where I was. There are a lot of women in middle management, but mostly it's men making decisions and filtering the material," Moses says. "While some programming is a science, some is taste. It's intuitive. If you're at ESPN, you don't see so many women because women aren't the primary watchers of sports. At Univision, there aren't a lot of white people programming because it caters to Hispanics. But when I look at the women's networks, there are still very few women doing creative work."

If this were true in her industry, where women are major consumers, then what was it like in other professions?

Moses wanted the chance to meet smart, determined women like herself, but she knew it wouldn't be easy. The gals she sought were already operating on overdrive, constantly flinging themselves across continents in pursuit of fulfillment, a quest for some greater piece of the pie. So she and Willow Bay were stunned when they reached out and, without fail, every woman said yes, and they were elated when a core group of about a dozen—including the founders of Juicy Couture, the co-owner of the L.A. Sparks WNBA team, and one of the few female cardiothoracic surgeons in the world—began to gel. "They didn't know these other women," Moses says, "but they found the idea very empowering."

> *"Being with these women, reaching out to others, we all end up talking about our personal stories and life journeys. It's pure magic and we're moved out of our universe for a couple of hours."—Kim Moses*

These ladies have met monthly for the past three years, and Moses is always there to greet them when they arrive. "They've had heavy days, long days, and there's such a look of excitement and anticipation," she continues. "Each time, new information comes out or something special opens up. It's never the same thing. Being with these women, reaching out to others, we all end up talking about our personal stories and life journeys. It's pure magic and we're moved out of our universe for a couple of hours."

The women call their cabal The Vault because they've come to truly know and trust each other. Everyone contributes and everyone is discreet, and they've learned that, like Moses, each one is self-made. "We talk about everything from employee issues to problems we're having with our husbands. It's not in the PTA–coffee klatch kind of way, but more sharing points of view on where the world is heading, what's happening to kids in our communities," Moses says. "It's having women at the table, talking and sharing and helping us figure out where to go next."

Moses and Bay invite special guests to ensure that each dinner has a distinctive slant and feels unique. Visitors, of course, aren't just any seat-fillers. They're women like Leslie Sanchez, the Republican political analyst; Judy Smith, a Washington, D.C.–based crisis manager (with clients like Monica Lewinsky) who inspired the ABC hit show *Scandal*; Nicole Feld, half of the first sister-team to produce Ringling Bros. and Barnum & Bailey Circus; Dr. Helene Gayle, the president and CEO of CARE USA, the world's leading international humanitarian organization; and Sharmeen Obaid Chinoy, the Pakistani-Canadian filmmaker who won a 2012 Oscar for her documentary, *Saving Face*. Not a slouch in this bunch.

"It's opened my world way beyond the industry I've worked in. I feel like I'd been asleep before I started this group," Moses expands. "Most of us are very insular, but we're living in a world that is dynamically connected and this is the most incredible time to come together. We all know we're going to learn something and help each other."

While there was never any express purpose, no desire to shake down other chicks for their contacts, Vault members have found that when you put a bunch of motivated ladies in the same room, exciting things happen. The women have counseled each other through job transitions, formed strategic collaborations, and facilitated book deals. In one instance, when filmmaker Chinoy mentioned her desire to create an animated series for Pakistani youth to convey the Taliban's negative influence, Moses introduced her to another gal in the Vault constellation, Darla Anderson. Anderson is the top female at Pixar, a company known for films like *Toy Story*, *Monsters, Inc.*, and *Cars*, and she holds the Guinness World Record for the highest average movie gross of any producer. "You couldn't ask for a more valuable mentor than Darla for Sharmeen," Moses says. "All this happens just through these dinners. When we put people together and say, 'Can you help this woman?' everyone in our group says, 'Yes, absolutely.' It's amazing."

And though The Vault was never meant to be self-serving, Moses has benefited personally in spectacular ways. Vault ladies keep Moses's thinking current and serve as sources for her annual "Point of View" document, a 200-page analysis of the economy and culture used to buttress content she's creating for TV and digital media the following year. Moses also partnered with her friend and fellow Vault member Veronika Kwan-Rubinek, who is president of international distribution at Warner Bros. Pictures, on an outreach program for the international opening of Clint Eastwood's 2010 movie *Hereafter*.

"I had just done *Ghost Whisperer*, which was about mediums, so I knew her audience. I thought I could help," Moses says. "Because we had our shows airing in 169 countries, we digitally reached out to our fan base. We engaged with people we thought would be interested in this fare—in this case, mediums and talking to the dead. We drove those eyeballs and got them to the movie theaters." The collaboration was so effective that Kwan-Rubinek hired Sander/Moses to create an app for *Happy Feet 2*. It was the most downloaded app in the history of Warner Bros.

"These things happen organically in an informal way, but they also happen formally at the table. We're constantly thinking about what we can do for each other. By the end of every dinner, we all have something we can do to further somebody else," says Moses, high from the sale of new shows to ABC and CBS. "I've always had a problem asking for help, but this isn't like making a cold call. You may be the one asking for help today, but tomorrow you're the one who's giving help. Today I bet I fielded four calls from women who were sent to me by somebody else. Times have changed and women are in a position to help each other and make a difference. There's momentum now, and we're stitched together tighter."

North to the Future

The Vault has been a revelation for Moses, upending a prevailing view of high-powered women in the workplace. "Tiger ladies" aren't meant to have generous spirits. They're supposed to claw each other's eyes out, stab each other in the back. How else could they have climbed corporate ladders and not just survived, but thrived?

The Vault was always different, perhaps—Moses thought— exceptional. It had to be the result of a rare and secret chemistry. Moses believed she'd found a singular recipe, a pocket of warmth in a kitchen in a house in a tough town called L.A. She never imagined this formula could be replicated or that groups like hers were coalescing in other cities. She never believed women could be uniting across industries, offering support and sounding boards, fueling each other's journeys and providing safe landings in places as far-flung as Anchorage, Alaska.

But women were coming together in Anchorage too, as Liane Pelletier can attest. She found them once she mustered the courage to venture, as the Alaska state motto says, "North to the Future," to become a CEO.

Pelletier hadn't known she wanted to be a chief executive until she said it aloud, onstage and in public. Because she was one of few women leaders at Sprint, the telecom giant based in Overland Park, Kansas, she routinely won a featured speaking slot at the company's annual "Take Our Daughters and Sons to Work" event. So, on a spring day in 2000, Pelletier ascended to the dais without papers or props to tell Sprint employees and their children why she loved her profession.

Pelletier led the corporate strategy and business development group and—together with her 100-person team, many of whom had PhDs—she kept her finger on the pulse of the telecom industry, tracking trends, competitors, and emerging regulations to position her firm for success. "We were the brainiac department. I had this incredibly smart group of folks who could eat numbers and provide context," she says now, passion evident in her voice. "It was an awesome job."

When it came time for questions, one girl—the daughter of a man in Pelletier's group—raised her hand. "If you weren't doing this, what else would you do?" she asked. Without pausing to reflect on her response, Pelletier shot back, "I'd want to be CEO." Standing in the spotlight before hundreds of colleagues in a packed auditorium, Pelletier explained why she thought leading companies was heroic and why she believed she was ready.

By that time she'd worked at Sprint for seventeen years, and Pelletier was the youngest person and first woman to report directly to the chairman and CEO, Bill Esrey. Esrey was one of Pelletier's key mentors, iconic and intimidating and "a real statesman kind of guy," and he'd led Pelletier on "an incredible rocketship ride" through the company. She'd worked in market and product development before being tapped as executive assistant to the president, Ron LeMay. In this 24-7 role with no set job description, Pelletier became one of six trouble-shooting mentees groomed to lead Sprint in the future.

After two years working nonstop for LeMay, Pelletier led strategy for Esrey, attending high-profile meetings and learning the art and science of mergers and acquisitions at a time when her industry was consolidating. "I popped into corporate center and the doors blew open. I got to look at the company through a portfolio lens,"

Pelletier says. "I'd do deep dives in other divisions, come back up, put it all in context. I had to generate points of view about where the company should be looking, heading. I was in a candy store and all the shelves were available."

But at the same time her career was thriving, Pelletier's marriage was collapsing. "Relationships crumble in strange ways, and the office was my escape," she says, remembering how Esrey supported her through a difficult divorce. "For months, Bill was the only one I told. He would come to the office early, as I did. I'd be at my desk working before anyone else showed up, and I'd break out crying because my life was shifting like this. He just had this uncanny sense. He'd pop his head in the room and we'd talk about the business or some big news story. He was such a big character in the company, but he was sensitive and gentle enough to be my backstop. He would say gently to me, 'If you get to feeling this way in a meeting and need to step out, I'll be your cover.' He offered really practical ways to get through a rugged time."

Sprint was a second home for Pelletier, so when both Esrey and LeMay were forced out in 2003 over a questionable tax shelter, she found herself adrift. "I looked left and right and saw a lot of men, a lot of competition. I had a staff role. I had done line work, and that's how people prepare to be CEO. I could do it," she says. "But when my two mentors left, I was saddened."

So that spring, when she received a call from a headhunter at the global recruiting firm Spencer Stuart to gauge her interest in a CEO job, Pelletier got chills. And when the recruiter mentioned where—Anchorage—she shuddered again. Two summers before, Pelletier had traveled with her husband on a small cruise ship to Wrangell–St. Elias National Park, the largest national park in the United States and the most remote in Alaska. She remembered sitting alone on the beach, staring at monolithic icebergs and wondering, *What can you do professionally in Alaska and still have this at your doorstep? This is the most beautiful place on earth, but how do people make a go of it here?*

"My words on the stage, the place I'd just visited, the stunning picture of that iceberg in my mind: It all came crashing down on me," she remembers. "I had this epiphany. I was going."

Alaska Communications Systems (ACS) had been formed four years earlier by "a classic 1950s manager" who had leveraged strong relationships to roll up local telephone properties across the state. But, Pelletier says, he was ill-equipped to steer the business through a competitive twenty-first century. "From a management standpoint he was invisible. He didn't meet with customers and employees. There was no go-forward business strategy."

The firm's board members courted Pelletier intensely for six months, and from afar she researched the firm, investigating its history and rivals. She spoke with ACS directors every few days, but before agreeing to sign on, she wanted to understand what was really happening inside this operation. For that she had to consult the man she was being hired to replace, a man who had been told only late in the process that he was being ousted. "It wasn't a warm or long conversation, and he didn't think I had what it took to manage the company," says Pelletier in her sweet, modulated voice. "All I need to hear is 'You can't do it.' That's what he told me, and I doubled down to prove otherwise."

Pelletier—who has short dark hair, bright brown eyes, and a tendency to say "heck"—had finalized her divorce by then and had never had children, so in some ways it was a blessing that she didn't have to convince anyone to join her. But it also meant she was heading to Alaska alone, in winter, not knowing a soul.

In October 2003, she loaded two huge duffel bags, "the kind you can put bodies in," with books and a lead crystal reading lamp, suits, and so many shoes. For the time being, she'd be living out of a hotel, and who knew when she'd have access to her storage space? Pelletier crammed it all in, everything she might need—including evening gowns, stilettos, and rhinestone sandals—and prepared to become a chief executive. She arrived in Anchorage on a rainy Friday night, and the head of human resources met her at the hangar and took her to a Residence Inn a block from the office. "There she was, helping me schlep all these shoes, many of which I never wore in Alaska," Pelletier laughs. "But it was part of my security blanket."

ACS would pack up her furniture and deliver it a month later, so there were only so many inaugural errands she could run, only so much provisioning she could do. On a previous visit, she'd driven past company headquarters, a municipally owned pile of gray cinderblocks she could describe simply as "gulag architecture," but she'd never been inside. Pelletier decided to head into the office the next day to get her bearings. New key-card in hand, she took a deep breath and entered. The building's nondescript, "hospital tan" walls and industrial carpet were a far cry from the rich woods and Oriental rugs she'd left behind at Sprint, and when Pelletier walked up four flights to her new office, she found it totally empty. There was nothing: no computer, no budget, no telephone list. Nothing, Pelletier recalls, save the scent of her predecessor's cologne. "It just felt very cold, and I wondered, 'Is this how people like things here?' There was not a lot of love applied to that company."

Pelletier then ventured to a car dealer to purchase the Land Rover a friend in Kansas City said would keep her safe on Alaska's icy roads. But when she told a salesman what model she wanted, he just smirked. He didn't have that brochure, much less the car. It was Alaska, lady, and the latest models didn't debut here. So much for "Altitude, Not Attitude," as the bumper stickers read.

Yet the day was bright and crisp and, if other attempts at nest building proved fruitless, at least Pelletier could buy herself a fur coat. She wasn't a fur lover, but Alaskans considered pelts a necessity to combat wicked winds. Alaskans wore their fur like armor, and with her new chocolate brown, ankle-length sheared beaver, Pelletier would be equipped to meet her troops the following night.

ACS's board of directors had asked its new CEO to come to the Marriott Hotel on Sunday evening to get acquainted with her management team, and Pelletier was hoping for a smooth transition. When she arrived at the designated conference room, French doors flung open and, like a new bride entering a banquet hall, Pelletier was announced with great flourish. It was only then—when the mingling stopped and everyone froze, and when her employees stared, stone-faced and dumbfounded—that Pelletier learned that no one had been told a new face would appear in the corner office Monday morning. Surprise!

"The person who planned it, it must have been the Marriott, had no clue about the backdrop," she says. "There was one long table and I sat in the middle and could speak to exactly three people. That didn't feel so good."

Though she commenced one-on-one meetings the next day, Pelletier says her employees remained complacent. She knew they felt challenged and abused, that no one had considered them, but in the end she couldn't summon their enthusiasm. "It was a very downbeat employee base. They hadn't felt a win in a long time. They weren't pulled together as a team," she sighs. "There was no fire in the belly, no interest to hit the restart button." A quick, steady turnover ensued until only one senior manager remained—the firm's general counsel, "which is great because you always want someone who knows what's in the closets."

Pelletier relied on her stocked Rolodex of friends and former colleagues to recruit superstars who could convince their families to move to Alaska. "I had a 100-day plan," she smiles, "and for the next 100 days, I planned the work and worked the plan." In addition to hiring, Pelletier met with the ACS's largest shareholders and customers, and with media, community groups, and the state regulatory commission. She tried to ingratiate herself with the Anchorage community, but this too proved difficult. "When Alaskans see newcomers arrive, they expect they're carpetbaggers who will make money and leave," she says. "My second week on the job, at an Anchorage Chamber of Commerce meeting, I mentioned I'd bought a house and I got a standing ovation. It was my first clue: To show Alaskans that you're a good guy, you need to invest in Alaska."

Pelletier needed to prove she was there to stay, but to call Alaska "the last frontier" was an understatement: She faced economic and cultural challenges she'd never anticipated. The state is more than twice the size of Texas with a population smaller than Austin's, and its economy is markedly different from that of the rest of the country. Pelletier says Alaska's $38 billion Permanent Fund, which distributes dividends mainly from oil producers to every state resident, has a discouraging effect on the working populace. "If you're a business-minded person like me, going to turn a company around, you're operating in an entitlement culture with lots of libertarians. It's off the grid and they like it that way, but at the same time they need all the developments happening in the lower forty-eight," she says. "It's a strange mix of 'get-out-of-my-face, but still send the money.'"

Pelletier got used to people calling her a "cheechako," or newbie, and she began to overhaul her new firm. She established a budget, which didn't exist when she stepped into her role, and set out to build Alaska's first statewide wireless network. During her tenure as CEO, Pelletier bought and built submarine cables to connect Alaska's networks to the lower forty-eight states and repurposed ACS's legacy residential telephone assets for business. And, from day one, she rehabilitated the company's culture. "We made it more customer-centric. We care about and measure customers," she says. "We break down our walls and think about end-to-end process. We cut across departments and ask questions, rather than reinforcing the silo mentality I walked into."

In the course of this transformation, Pelletier also realized ACS needed a new board, as the firm's fresh strategy required skills and experience its current directors lacked. Because many local corporations are run by Alaska Native women, Pelletier began to make cold calls, introducing herself to herald the changes she was making and to ask the women to recommend potential directors. By then, Pelletier had weathered enough long, dark winters to be deemed a "sourdough," or survivor—which meant the ladies actually took her calls.

Anchorage is a small community, and the same people tend to sit on boards and attend black-tie dinners. By calling and showing up, Pelletier eventually met the influential women in town, and slowly she was accepted. Once she'd graduated from a cheechako to a sourdough, Pelletier discovered women there to help her succeed, and one defining day these ladies took seats around a very big table.

Pelletier and other women from Anchorage began convening to pursue their separate and common goals. Some were Alaska Natives, while others were transplants, but all were sourdoughs with a proven commitment to the state economy. Once a month, Betsy

Lawer, the president of the First National Bank of Alaska, would open her boardroom and about a dozen community and business leaders—all female—would file in. Members included a lawyer in Senator Lisa Murkowski's office; the chancellor of the University of Alaska Anchorage, who now chairs the U.S. Arctic Research Commission; the superintendent of the Anchorage School District; and senior executives at BP Alaska and Alaska Airlines.

For an hour and fifteen minutes, the women delivered updates on their diverse areas of expertise. "We went around the table. They'd say, 'What's up in the telecom space, Liane?' and I'd give my description. Then Betsy would tell us what the housing market was doing," Pelletier says. "I've been around men most of my life and they shoot the breeze, but we were so purposeful about picking each other's brains. We'd just go at it and we were extremely efficient. It felt like we solved the world's issues in an hour."

> *The last few years have seen an explosion of women's groups like The Vault and 4C2B. Formidable ladies across professions are convening at unprecedented rates, forming salons, dinner groups, and networking circles, and collaborating to achieve clout and success.*

Job creation and the oil and gas industry were always central to the discussion, and the women would advocate together when the legislature met in Juneau. Quietly, they wielded their collective influence in the state. And while they weren't there to socialize, sometimes they'd wink and whisper that old saw about men in town: *The odds are good, but the goods are odd.*

"We would decide ahead of time if it would be just us chickens, or if we would have a guest like the governor or the head of

ConocoPhillips, whom we would grill on issues," says Pelletier. "Invited guests, mostly guys, would walk into the room and say, 'Oh my God. I didn't realize you all knew each other!'"

In e-mails, the ladies called themselves "4C2B"—"Force to Be," as in "reckoned with." 4C2B bounced around ideas, circulated job opportunities on a private distribution list, and helped each woman gain a competitive advantage in her field. Some of its participants were key clients of ACS, and Pelletier says 4C2B helped her establish relationships and develop insights into her customer base. "Through these relationships, I was able to show that the ACS they used to know, which was rigid and monopolistic, was now service-oriented," she says. "I used that platform to educate them, and I know they helped spread the word. We all did that for each other."

Ultimately, Pelletier spent seven-and-a-half years at ACS, and she groomed her successor before moving to Seattle to become a professional corporate director. Now that she's back in the lower forty-eight, Pelletier smiles when recalling that girl in the audience at Sprint who asked what she wanted to do next. When Pelletier decided to leave Sprint for ACS, the girl's father came home and told his family over dinner. "That's great!" the girl exclaimed. "Don't you remember she wanted to be a CEO?"

"It wasn't my employee, but his daughter who remembered," Pelletier says. "He wrote an e-mail to tell me, and I printed and kept it. She's now in college and from what I understand, she's quite a rock star."

Playing the Gender Card

It wasn't that Pelletier had never experienced professional support from women. There was one other female in her "Leadership Challenge" class, as the Sprint bench of six were called, and the two made a pact to share promotion and compensation details, and to help each other script difficult conversations for as long as they worked as colleagues. But it was only when she left the comfort of Kansas that Pelletier found strength in numbers. 4C2B women were drawn from different arenas, and through the sheer breadth of their expertise and connections, they could affect large-scale change.

In the past, women like Pelletier had few outlets for their concerns as they rose in their careers. They relied on supportive male mentors like Esrey and LeMay and they sought other gals for friendship, but they didn't expect their girlfriends to further their careers. So, like Kim Moses, Pelletier never envisioned groups like hers springing up across the nation, and she'd certainly never heard about The Vault.

But the last few years have seen an explosion of women's groups like The Vault and 4C2B. Formidable ladies across professions are convening at unprecedented rates, forming salons, dinner groups, and networking circles, and collaborating to achieve clout and success. Their coteries often have tongue-in-cheek names—like SLUTS (Successful Ladies Under Tremendous Stress) in New York, or the VIEW (Very Important Executive Women) in Atlanta, or Brazen Hussies, which convenes women across regions—and their goals are the same: purposeful mingling among equals.

Suddenly, it seems, women who would never prioritize the sisterhood are finding themselves in a sea of doppelgangers. Women who wouldn't deign to "play the gender card," much less use that dowdy, dated "f-word"—*feminism*—are discovering ways to connect and advance one another professionally. They are now doing deals not because of affirmative action or an altruistic intent to lift up the gender, but because it is smart business with people they know and trust. Their informal relationships are resulting in billions of dollars of transactions, corporate board seats attained, promotions landed, and companies formed and funded. *For the first time in history, women are seeing a monetary return on time invested with girlfriends.*

The next decade will see an explosion of female wealth and power. But it's not about the money, women say. It's about the love. There's a massive money trail, but the relationships themselves are not transactional; they're true friendships based in loyalty, care, and respect. And in nearly every case, women trace triumphs to a simple query:

"How can I help?"

CHAPTER 2

LADIES WHO LUNCH

omen are building cross-sector networks in Los Angeles and Anchorage, New York and Atlanta, ostensibly in a vacuum. Like Kim Moses and Liane Pelletier, these gals haven't yet realized that their counterparts around the country are doing the same, or that their groups—"Stiletto Networks"—increasingly intersect, sparking a powerful nationwide trend.

As a result, many of the top women in technology now know the top women in finance, who know the top women in media, who know the top women in law, who know the top women in retail, and so on. By reaching horizontally across industry silos, businesswomen have redefined critical mass. They've thrown the net wider, and from this new perspective, there are suddenly many more ladies with whom to affiliate.

Recently, even women within the same professions, sometimes direct competitors, have begun to assemble to share intelligence and find ways to excel. They are pushing each other to be better and do more, and in the process they are changing the dynamics of industries in which they work.

Hello Wrinkles, Good-Bye Job

Network TV news is the last place one might expect this to happen. It's notoriously ruthless and bitchy, one big popularity contest where "likeability" is based on looks rather than competence. It's tough for female anchors to focus on the job when viewers zero in on their crow's-feet and when camera time is fleeting no matter how strong their journalistic cred. Hello wrinkles, good-bye job.

Kitty Pilgrim knew this only too well, and she'd managed to last well past most female anchors' expiration date at age 40. She'd begun her career at CNN as a producer, but she was identified as anchor material when higher-ups saw she was not only clever and articulate but also gorgeous. Even now, more than a decade later, Pilgrim turns heads. The dark, shiny hair. The mesmerizing green eyes. The pale, creamy skin. After winning Emmy, Peabody, and Overseas Press Club awards, and after twenty-five years reporting on countries in seismic transition—covering weighty topics like the economic rise of China, the first free elections in South Africa, and the collapse of the Soviet Union—"Kitty Pilgrim legs" precedes her bio as a Google search.

Still, Pilgrim insists she wasn't interested in being on camera. "I was interested in the stories," she says, "but they said, 'Too bad.'" In an attempt to minimize distractions and concentrate on reporting, Pilgrim would buy twelve suits every season and label them numerically, rotating each day to ensure she didn't repeat the same outfit on air too soon. She encouraged other women to do the same.

"I can tell immediately who's going to succeed and who's not," she says. "I can tell when a reporter's going to fail, if she's too into the shoes, hair, and makeup. The kids who come through my office with stars in their eyes who say, 'I want to be on TV!' I've said, 'You'll never make it because you don't care about reporting the story.' It has to be about the story. I love being feminine, but you can't make that your job."

For her own sanity, Pilgrim had to stay centered. When her boys were one and three years old, she'd left their father and won sole custody and decision making, so she was raising them completely alone. Sure, she needed money, but she also had to be happy and emotionally present at home, and she couldn't do that if every day were a fight. "I'm not a competitive person. I hate competition. I'm much more collaborative," she says. "I never felt I had to compete with someone sitting next to me. I compare myself to myself. Was the program I just produced better or worse than the one I produced before? If I spent my day looking over my shoulder at who's coming up behind me, I'd be miserable."

Plus, Pilgrim says, in her experience, backstabbing women don't get very far. Of course, there are catty girls and ones who sleep their way to the top, but in the end it's about proficiency. "Competition won't teach you skills, and no one can hand them to you," she says. "You have to learn those on your own."

Pilgrim knew that experience is the currency of journalism, so opportunities to expand knowledge are key. She worked to hone her own skills and, according to women who've worked with her, she always helped build the skills of others. As a fellow at the East-West Center, a think tank in Honolulu, she heard about scholarships or fellowships that might benefit underlings in her newsroom, and she recommended and provided references for six young women at CNN to go to Asia for a five-week trip. Each one would return an expert in her field.

Pilgrim was celebrated as a nice girl and a superstar in her trade, but all the skills in the world couldn't stop her ticking clock. "It's worse in media because it's all appearance-based," she says, recalling a time when CNN's former top dog, Ted Turner, returned to the set as a guest on Pilgrim's show, *Lou Dobbs Tonight*. She'd known Turner for years by then and he'd been her great fan and supporter, but that day he was telling it straight: Her days were numbered. "He said, 'Kitty, you must be shaking in your boots! You're almost forty. They're not going to let you stay much longer,'" Pilgrim remembers. "And I said, 'No, Ted, you're wrong. I'll tell you the truth. I'm over fifty.'"

Though she was at the pinnacle of her career, Pilgrim had already orchestrated her second act writing international thrillers with a daring female protagonist. So she became a cheerleader among her female colleagues after CNN began downsizing and *Lou Dobbs Tonight* was canceled in 2009. In the nine months that followed, Pilgrim rallied five women who'd worked at CNN to meet for lunch for as long as they were unemployed. The ladies hosted elaborate catered feasts at home or made reservations at trendy restaurants so that, at least once a month, they could dress up and feel good about themselves. "We just thought, 'We're not all going to crawl off and be miserable,'" Pilgrim says. "We spent so much time at work enjoying each other's company, and that's what we were really missing."

Ironically, the women called it their "Ladies Who Lunch" club, because never in their entire working lives had they indulged in lingering midday meals. Their first repast was at Michael's, the media haunt in midtown Manhattan where, instead of shrinking back in sweatpants, they donned stilettos and sauntered into a pen of their high-powered peers.

The Ladies Who Lunch discussed opportunities and who was hiring, and they worked to multiply their individual connections. "I had already planned my transition, but for some it was harder,"

Pilgrim says. "We found that five people looking are so much more efficient than one. Together we could scope the entire industry."

One afternoon, Pilgrim organized a lunch at the Park Avenue penthouse she shares with Maurice Tempelsman, the mogul she met on the Council on Foreign Relations. Though he's been Pilgrim's loyal partner for years, many still recognize Tempelsman as the long-term companion of former First Lady Jacqueline Kennedy Onassis. Obviously, he has fine taste in women, but Tempelsman was nowhere to be seen as the Ladies Who Lunch sipped wine on the terrace, then moved indoors for a four-course extravaganza served on china with Christofle silver and Waterford crystal.

> These gals might not have seen a bright future at CNN, but still they were a team. They faced life events together because they weren't just colleagues. They were friends.

That day, the women were also fêting a colleague in her final days of pregnancy, and after polishing off her lemon tart, the mother-to-be excused herself to go to the bathroom. When she emerged minutes later, clearly something was up. Apparently Pilgrim's corn and jalapeño soup had done the trick, and it was time to call her doctor! "We joked that we're so tough, we finish all our courses before we go into labor," Pilgrim laughs. The Ladies Who Lunch took pictures and piled presents into a taxi. Their colleague left for the hospital in a torrent of bags and bows, waves and good wishes and love.

These gals might not have seen a bright future at CNN, but still they were a team. Still, they faced life events together because they weren't just colleagues. They were friends. And all the women eventually landed on their feet, finding jobs as executive producers, anchors, and correspondents—or, like Pilgrim, the courage to change course entirely.

"Kitty is smart as hell, and she's the shining example of *good guys win*," says her friend Jenny Rider, who is now a communications consultant and executive speechwriter. Rider worked with Pilgrim at CNN, and though she left long ago, she and Pilgrim have continued to support each other through job changes, raises, and promotions. "She cares how I'm doing, where I end up. She's always been someone I could call and say, 'Here's where I am with my business, this is what I need,' and I've helped her too because her success is just as important to me. I don't know why she's so generous with her time in an industry renowned for being cutthroat, but it's made a big difference in my career. It's just the way she rolls.

"It might sound cheesy, but these groups are real families. It's always 'How can I help?' and 'What can I do for you?' in a loving way," Rider continues. "You may not see each other for a while, but you know people care and are looking out for you. It's family."

From Victim to Fixer

Joan Lau already had a family—a compassionate partner and young daughter—and she didn't think she needed one at work. But when she found herself in crisis, women came forward to help her, and she discovered what she'd never thought possible: sisters-in-arms who pressed Lau to step out of a boss's shadow and rocket her career in a new direction. They made her believe she could do it, even in biotech, a field nearly devoid of women.

Lau had labored for eight years at Merck, the healthcare mammoth, in R&D, project management, and corporate business development. In these roles she was visible to senior staff, but she wasn't a leader herself. In her own words, she was a back-office, chief-of-staff kind of gal—strictly middle management.

One of Lau's jobs was to drive drug development projects, including oncology programs where she worked with MD/PhDs like Jamie Freedman. Freedman was a big thinker, creative and impulsive, and Lau, with her gift for steady execution, was his perfect foil. So when Freedman left Merck to become the chief medical officer of Locus Pharmaceuticals, just five minutes from the Merck office in the Philadelphia suburbs, the two kept in touch. Within a year, Freedman was in the CEO seat, cleaning house; with his board's support, he let go of every member of Locus's senior leadership team with hope of reviving the flagging company. Now he wanted Lau to be his right hand.

Lau had heard the rumors. She knew Locus was struggling. But Freedman inspired her and she saw an opportunity to learn and stretch. "Jamie and I had experience at Merck doing very challenging things and having greater than average success," Lau remembers. "Jamie worked incredibly hard, and I enjoyed finding ways to help realize his creative and innovative ideas."

People in biotech need passion and faith, Lau says, because so much of their time is spent trying to beat seemingly insurmountable odds, as the chance of any drug making it from clinical studies into the market is remarkably small. "Jamie had passion and I wanted nothing more than to work with someone with that much energy," she continues. "I trusted when he said an idea was good. I wanted to go against those odds."

Lau, a comfortable cog in the big pharma wheel, quit her job at Merck to become Freedman's COO. She arrived at Locus on June 1, 2009, and four days later, Freedman pulled her into his office. "Spill it," Lau urged when she saw her friend pacing. Freedman said he'd received an offer from another firm, and while he'd been vacillating for days, he had finally decided to take it. He was moving to Miami.

"Are you fucking kidding me?" Lau lost her signature cool. She wanted to know how and when. Was he sure? Had Freedman consulted his wife? Had he told their chairman? How could he do this to her?

"My jaw dropped. I hadn't even met the board yet," Lau recounts, still incredulous. "He left about a week later, and because he had let everyone go before I got there, the only person left was a two-day-a-week, part-time CFO who worked as a consultant. The only officer of the company was me."

Everyone scrambled. Locus's board appointed Lau president immediately, and a few months later bestowed the CEO title as well. Lau—who was in her late thirties and had never managed more than eight employees, had never run a major division (much less a company), and knew nothing of the start-up and venture capital worlds—was now at the helm of a sinking ship.

In those first, nerve-wracking days, Lau developed an action plan and tried not to panic, but it would be months before she could sleep again. She began working every night until midnight, when she'd collapse in bed, mind still racing. What had she done, and how would this affect her family? Lau would doze, then wake suddenly at 2 or 3 AM and return to her computer. "I went into intense overdrive. It disturbed a lot of the employees because they were getting e-mails from me at 2 AM, but not just at 2. They'd also get them at 3 and 4 and 5," Lau says now. "I wasn't a chemist, and this was a chemistry company. I had so much to learn. Jamie brought me in because he was overwhelmed by the amount of work he had to do. It was the justification for hiring me, and now that was all on me. I had a serious insomnia problem."

Before she'd accepted Freedman's offer, Lau had the foresight to make contacts outside Merck. She sought a broader network to help learn about the start-up sphere she was stepping into, and Wharton, where she'd completed her executive MBA, seemed a good place to start. Lau had called Gloria Rabinowitz, a 1978 Wharton business school graduate who led the Wharton Alumni Club of Philadelphia, and Rabinowitz opened doors, introducing Lau to female entrepreneurs.

"I originally reached out because I wanted to learn how to be a good biotech COO, but on my fourth day of work I called her and said, 'Scratch that, I have a different need now,'" Lau recalls. "I'm sure there was shock and panic in my voice."

Rabinowitz leapt into action. She insisted Lau join her at a meeting of the Alliance of Women Entrepreneurs (AWE), where she promised Lau would meet everyone she needed to know, people who could help her. Lau had heard about AWE for years, but resisted joining because she figured it was a holding tank for the "cookie and brownie" crowd, women with side-businesses who wouldn't relate to her exigency and concerns. But Rabinowitz tsk-tsked, and Lau arranged to come as her guest.

Lau is an introvert who hates networking, so forcing small talk in crowded spaces is agony for her. "My desperation was so high that I got on my business suit and loitered at the front desk until she arrived," she says. "Gloria dragged me to this event in a law office conference room, and when she arrived she hooked my arm." The two women would navigate the room together.

At that point, Lau knew Locus Pharmaceuticals had taken a lot of venture capital—$120 million—and had very few assets left. She knew the company name carried negative connotations, and Merck colleagues had advised her to change it when she arrived. "People did say negative things, but when you work in middle management at Merck, you don't know about the VC world or small biotechs," Lau sighs. "You're not tapped in." She never could have anticipated the visceral reaction women would have when they saw "Locus Pharmaceuticals" on her name tag that night.

When Rabinowitz introduced Lau to Jane Hollingsworth, a founder and the CEO of the neuroscience concern NuPathe and one of the most accomplished executives in her domain, Hollingsworth took one look at Lau's name tag and rolled her eyes. "I made a comment like, 'I've never had an introduction go like *this* before,'" Lau says. Yet Rabinowitz came to her rescue, exhorting Hollingsworth to hear Lau's story.

"Jane looks at me and her jaw drops too. If *Candid Camera* came out, she wouldn't have been surprised," Lau laughs. But then Hollingsworth engaged, asking Lau about her background, how this had happened, and how she could help. "We talked about what I wanted to do with Jamie's strategy, which she thought might actually have a shot," she continues. "Jane said, 'That's the first time I've heard something reasonable from a Locus employee.'"

Rabinowitz scurried off to find more women for Lau to meet, while Lau strained to carry a conversation on her own. "I don't talk well, so it always wraps up early" she says. "But Gloria came over again and hooked my arm." Rabinowitz had cobbled together a group of women in biotech, including the headhunter who'd moved Freedman to Locus. As Lau struggled to shoot the breeze, she saw Hollingsworth out of the corner of her eye. Hollingsworth's back was to Lau and she was chatting with another group when suddenly, all four women looked over and started laughing.

A decade before, Locus had been touted as the next big thing in pharma, a predicted pacesetter like Amgen, but Lau learned quickly that her company was now the butt of jokes. Against these headwinds, she felt an overwhelming burden. Had she just ruined her career?

Rabinowitz walked her to the parking lot. "You'll be fine," she assured Lau. "These women will contact you." And they did. Each one, including Jane Hollingsworth, requested a meeting. Hollingsworth spent nearly three hours at lunch reviewing Locus's strategy, and two headhunters called to see how they could fill the company's ranks. The women then contacted their friends, including four CEOs of other biotech companies, potential competitors who also reached out to ask: *How can I help?*

"They put guardrails around me. I created a network overnight," Lau says, still amazed. "Not a single one had another motive other than to help me out. Three of them hounded me to join AWE. They get no bonus for recruiting new members, but of course I joined because they all believed it was so valuable."

Lau had no clue how to manage large-scale personnel issues, much less a board of frustrated venture capitalists, but her peers offered insider knowledge of industry dynamics. They advised Lau on everything from mundane scientific minutiae to how to motivate her troops, and when Lau needed an auditor, biotech lawyer, and investment banking contacts, the women teed them up. They called to establish context in advance so Lau's appeals would be met with understanding.

"These women who were so busy always met with me. A couple times, Jane would randomly call me to see how I was doing," Lau says. "They all say, 'Let's have lunch or breakfast,' 'Come join my table at an event.'" Other women, powerful female VCs familiar with the Locus minefield, assisted Lau with strategy. They knew her board members personally, so they helped Lau isolate their triggers. They described the venture capitalists' motivation and personalities, explaining why each one had initially invested in Locus and what each expected in return. The women armed Lau with everything she needed to deliver.

"At Merck you can get mentors, but at the end of the day it's all for Merck. But these biotech women essentially compete for the same dollars in the same industry I do. My company was so bad off, they probably didn't think of it as competition, but they poured their hearts out for me," Lau says. "If I wrote an e-mail right now and said I need fifteen minutes tomorrow, I could get 99 percent of them. And the 1 percent who didn't respond, it would be because she's in Japan. They receive no benefit, but they helped me every step of the way."

Jane Hollingsworth says that if Lau felt anxious at that first AWE event, she didn't let it show. Lau was clearly in a tough spot, but she never broke character as a consummate professional. And, Hollingsworth figured, if Lau had the backing of a respected woman like Gloria Rabinowitz, then she had to be first-rate. "I knew what she had gotten herself into better than she did, that her situation was worse than most. I knew if she was willing to take my help, I had to help her," Hollingsworth says. "I wanted to help Gloria, so if Gloria wants me to help her, I'm helping Gloria too. It goes around.

"Biotech is growing and pharma is shrinking," Hollingsworth continues. "One of my big goals is to bubble up some of these businesses, to help interested people get into it. Joan is incredibly talented, she's respectful of everyone's time, and she was willing to do this. Obviously, we have our own businesses to run and we do the best we can, but it's much more fulfilling to think more broadly than that. I like the idea that I now have—through the years of success and a lot of pain—learned some things. Why should I just sit on that? I might as well let some people benefit from it."

When Lau arrived at Locus, the company had nine months of funding left, or six months if Lau wanted to close with enough runway to be even slightly attractive to potential buyers. Yet with the advice of her mentors, she made Locus's money last more than a year. She embarked on a couple of skunkworks projects—low-cost, possibly high-reward side efforts that might yield hope for the future. And when Locus began to run out of money, her board members saw enough potential in the skunkworks to extend their funding another year.

While her team never saw a "hit," Lau says they got the products far enough that a buyer could assume responsibility. "At the end of the day, my board is all men and they recognized the situation was tough, but given the circumstances it came out okay," says Lau, who again sought advice from her posse for the company's sale. "It's not a billion-dollar company, but it turned out better than anyone expected."

> Before she bonded with these women, Lau had fretted about fitting in. Other biotech CEOs seemed cut from the same cloth: white Republican men in their sixties who drink and play golf.

Even before Lau closed Locus operations in May 2011, her ladies started goading her to consider her next move. All those warroom tête-à-têtes had provided insight into Lau's character, her willingness to suppress her ego, and her ability to remain calm as she marched step-by-step toward a turnaround no one had believed was possible. As Lau's time at Locus came to a close, venture capitalists appeared from the wings. "One said she was impressed with how I had thought through a lot of the pieces. One of her companies had a drug program they had high hopes for, but the board member and CEO were at a standstill," Lau says with pride. "I said, 'I'm busy now, but when I'm done with Locus I'll come over and right that ship.'"

Before she bonded with these women, Lau had fretted about fitting in. Other biotech CEOs seemed cut from the same cloth: white Republican men in their sixties who drink and play golf. When Lau attended industry events, everyone assumed she was a spouse. "I'm just extremely different. I'm not straight, I'm not white, I'm not old, and I'm not male. I don't drink because my enzymes don't work. For a while I thought [that] since I can't fix these other things about me, maybe I can play golf," she says. "Remember in the 1980s when women wore those dorky silk ties? They were all trying to be men. Playing golf would have been more of the same, but now I know there's a better forum."

It took guidance and pressure from other ladies to push Lau from a timid middle manager to a confident, sought-after CEO employing her steady hand to bring companies back from the brink. A woman who began as a victim and emerged as a fixer, she is now the president and CEO of Azelon Pharmaceuticals. "I was at Azelon before I'd even had an opportunity to put together a résumé," she beams. "Of course I called Jane and the others. Everyone knew about this company, and this time I knew more about it too. I learned so much at Locus and now I'm extremely focused. I went in much better. I still can't believe my good fortune."

No "Kumbaya" Girls Here

Sometimes it takes an extreme case like Lau's or a transition point like Pilgrim's to bring women together. Other times, it's something smaller, like an item in the news, that galvanizes a group. In 2007, when an article appeared in now-defunct *Portfolio* magazine claiming that only a handful of women were true deal makers in private equity, "it made people furious," says Kelly Williams, a managing director at Credit Suisse who leads the bank's customized fund investment group, a $27 billion business that invests in private equity and venture capital firms. "We said we needed to develop a formal network. Women tend to get together for cocktails, but we needed something more organized."

After passing on the name Women In Private Equity (WIPE) for obvious reasons, Williams, who is based in New York, helped launch the Private Equity Women Investor Network (PE WIN) to be a resource for senior women in her field. She believed the 180 female managing directors, partners, chief investment officers, and senior portfolio managers across various firms needed to know each other. The group aims to share investment ideas, open channels for women to co-invest, and raise the profile of women leaders both within and outside the industry. "If you want to learn about distressed debt, you can call a woman," Williams says. "Many people in the industry don't know there are women who are deep experts in some of these fields."

Women in the network are expected to draw upon the authority their collective imparts, and when a member of PE WIN reaches out to Williams, she always returns the call. "The fact that she can get a call back from me gives her power in her own partnership. It changes the dynamics within her firm to have a more intimate relationship with the investor," says Williams, who was named by *American Banker* magazine as one of the "25 Most Powerful Women in Finance" in 2011. "We need to make sure that the women partners in those firms get invested in that power."

Williams says these things happen naturally for men all the time. "They run into their buddies five times in the hallway and they don't think twice about calling. Women have to make special appointments to get together," she expands. "It's a newer experience for women, but I'm seeing it happen in the network."

Similarly, Mallun Yen is seeing—and making—it happen in law. Yen says that in 2005, when she was tapped to lead the worldwide intellectual property (IP) legal department at Cisco Systems, the world's largest producer of computer networking equipment, she could count on one hand the number of senior women in her field. IP generally requires science and engineering degrees, where men vastly outnumber women, even in Silicon Valley.

Yen decided to contact her female counterparts at companies like Google, Atmel, Cadence, Sun, Intuit, and eBay, and the women began meeting up. "We didn't exactly know why, but we've found that having a peer group and supporting each other makes us better at what we're doing," she says. "Now there are seven of us who were all heads of IP at different companies. There's so little socializing between women at different firms and the field is so male-dominated, so it's really satisfying."

At times the ladies of ChIPs, which is short for "Chiefs in IP," have found themselves in heated professional disputes against one another. Their companies might be embroiled in a bitter patent war, but they remain friendly. "We get to the end result faster than if we had no relationships or trust," Yen says.

As the members of ChIPs have ascended together in their careers, they've been each other's confidantes and helped each other make certain leaps. In 2010, Yen left Cisco to become an executive vice president of corporate development at RPX, a provider of patent risk solutions, and many of these women became her clients. "It's not commiseration about how few women there are in IP. These are not 'kumbaya' women who sit around. They're really smart and they've worked really hard to get where they are, especially because they're women. So it's about making introductions, making sure you get the meeting, helping you and your company to be successful."

And Yen has been successful. RPX was in its nascency when the company's CEO visited to run an idea by Yen. "Two minutes into their pitch, I stopped them and said it's a great idea, you have to do it, it'll be incredibly successful, Cisco will be your first customer, and I'll help you work on making it successful," she says. RPX scored funding from legendary VC John Doerr at Kleiner Perkins and was profitable from year one. Within slightly more than two years, RPX broke $100 million in revenue, making it one of the fastest-growing start-ups in history, and when the company went public in May 2011, it was valued at nearly $1 billion.

Yen credits ChIPs with consistently supporting her venture and greasing the wheels in invaluable ways. "They say, 'Who do you need to meet with here?' They want to hear about new ideas I'm bringing because it's going to help them, but also because it's me," she says. "Obviously they're going to make good business decisions, but because they know me and my abilities, they're going to listen."

Each ChIP looks out for the ladies in other ways, too. If a journalist wants an interview, or someone asks a member to keynote a conference, or someone seeks help with a deal, a ChIP refers the request to another woman if she can't fulfill it herself.

And they've bonded emotionally in a manner Yen didn't anticipate. Yen was in her mid-thirties, on maternity leave after the birth of her first child, when she was offered the "reach" job at Cisco. Paradoxically, she used the promotion as a chance to affirm her priorities. "I said I can't fly to China on half a day's notice. I need to make sure I see my children," she says. "I didn't have a baby to not see him grow up." As she assumed new roles, both professionally and personally, it was comforting to have female friends grappling with the same things.

Now Yen enjoys time with the children of other ChIPs too, as their support system extends well beyond work. "We've passed on maternity clothes, thrown each other's wedding and baby showers. We have barbecues. I have another ChIP's son's play set in our backyard! We all know each other's kids and I like their families," she says. "Every ChIP has ended up being very successful. We were all promoted to VP or became general counsel in our firms. Our responsibilities have gotten broader with promotions, bigger titles, and we've done it together. I can't say ChIPs is the cause, but there's something so special about these women."

ChIPs now realize they can influence the wider legal community too. "It's not just about helping ourselves, and it's not just mentoring here and there," Yen says. "We've learned we have an ability to send a message to law firms." Because, Yen says, heads of IP at major companies control the hundreds of millions of dollars their companies spend in legal fees every year, they can also have a say in the composition of legal teams.

> *"It's not just about helping ourselves, and it's not just mentoring here and there. We've learned we have an ability to send a message to law firms." —Mallun Yen*

"We believe having diverse teams makes us more effective. We've all experienced pitches from teams of five men, and we're just saying, 'Can't you do better?' It's not about having the token woman on the pitch because that's always so apparent. It's about asking partners why women aren't core parts of their teams. We ask those questions and we make sure law firms understand diversity results in a better defense or a stronger case."

When Yen sees a promising young woman on a team, she starts calling her to check in. "I say, 'How are they treating you? I know it's hard. I was in your spot.'" And Yen doesn't stop there; she also calls the woman's partners to make sure they're keeping her fulfilled and excited in her career. "I say, 'You know what she's trying to do is different, don't you? You know it's harder when you don't have any role models in the firm. What are you doing to give her adequate opportunities and not burn her out?' You want to make sure she's in for the long haul," continues Yen, who is now in her early forties. "A lot of these firms are still run by men and sometimes they're not sure how to relate, to make sure they're retaining women. So as senior women in our field, ChIPs now have the platform. We should use our influence to change these firms in a way that will benefit everyone."

ChIPs are starting to see the young women they've mentored achieve in their own right, which Yen says is "enormously gratifying." A number of women that ChIPs have championed have become the first women partners in IP at their firms, and the ChIPs network is expanding because other attorneys are eager to join. ChIPs core members make time for these aspirants, and they host regular events for 80 to 100 women (and sometimes a few men). One panel featured six female general counsels at public companies, while another included four female federal judges. In October 2012, ChIPs held its first major Women in IP National Summit in Washington, D.C. Some 250 women participated, including all four female Federal Circuit judges, marking the first time these women had ever convened on a panel.

"Our little idea snowballed," Yen says. "It's really unprecedented to have all these women gathered together in one room, women in

IP from diverse industries like tech, manufacturing, retail, medical devices, financial services, automotive, plus academia and all branches of the government."

A number of law firms offered generous sponsorship and support for the event, but rather than take money from any company, ChIPs required interested parties to submit an application stating how their firms demonstrated a commitment to female retention and advancement. "When I told one man he needed to fill out the application, he responded, 'This is the first time I've ever had to interview to write a check!'" Yen smiles. "But that's how we are different."

ChIPs gatherings are decidedly professional, yet conversations veer toward the personal too. "We'll talk about our own experiences. We end up sharing more than we would in another forum because it's smaller," Yen says and spontaneously starts laughing. At one particular event, a redoubtable federal judge was asked to recount her best court story. She leaned in conspiratorially and told the crowd that one day, her deputy, also a woman, approached her in chambers. A lawyer who'd just appeared in court had slipped her a note. "He wants to ask you out," the deputy whispered. At first the judge recoiled, but her deputy chided her to reconsider. The lawyer was *really* cute. "The judge eventually went out with him, and guess who's her husband now!" Yen exclaims before getting back to business. "We're not gender-specific. We don't spend time talking about work/life balance. It's intentionally more productive. But it was amazing and important to see this respected judge open up like that."

ChIPs are intense highfliers, but they're also human. They let down their guards for each other, and for other women. They think it's important to see the whole package—not to save one face for work and another for home—and their relationships are stronger because they're based on trust.

Whatever the impetus, women from law and finance and biotech and TV are realizing that campaigning on each other's behalf can be game-changing not only for the individuals involved, but also for companies—and soon, for entire professions. Thus far, women have been operating behind the scenes, but their groups are beginning to come to the fore, to assert themselves in ways that will revolutionize even stalwart industries in the decade to come.

"A lot of us woke up one day realizing we were now in a position to help others. Early in our careers, we just focused on working really hard, but then we poked our heads up and said, 'Hey, we've actually achieved something here,'" Yen says. "Now we can influence others and make a difference."

EVEN A LIVE
WIRE NEEDS
A CONNECTION

T he greatest beneficiaries of executive women's networks may be promising junior colleagues, many of whom are choosing entrepreneurship over corporate life. More and more, young women graduating college are eschewing a traditional path. Even a decade ago, girl go-getters would have tied long hair in tight ponytails, donned black Ann Taylor suits, low pumps, and a safe set of pearls, and lined up at Career Services for speed-round interviews. They would have prayed for temperature-controlled rooms so their palms would stay dry in firm handshakes—or at least to be spared the clammy digits of balding men in Hermes ties from McKinsey, Bain, Merrill Lynch, and Morgan Stanley. These hands, they knew, held the keys to their futures.

The lucky ones would have joined white-shoe bastions and, once there, they would hope to work for men with daughters, men who might see their children's future in the fresh-faced female analysts pulling all-nighters before client presentations. These girls would have pretended not to listen as their bosses explained to their stay-at-home wives that no, they wouldn't be home again tonight. And, especially if they were pretty, they'd be smart about hiding their femininity. They knew what could happen after so many late nights at the office.

But now the financial crisis has obliterated Wall Street jobs. The likelihood of landing plum positions is ever more slim, and "Occupy" movements on the nation's premier campuses have cast these professions in a dirty light. Grinding 100-hour weeks reworking Excel spreadsheets are infinitely less sexy when there's no higher purpose and no pot of gold.

As a result, the same Type A's who a generation ago would have spent years fighting to make partner are now reevaluating. These girls aim high. They're willing to work. But if they're going to sacrifice sleep and friends and lovers and families, why should it be for "The Man"? Why not have equity, some real skin in the game? Many know at least one peer who made fast money founding or joining a start-up. They don't have kids or *real* responsibilities yet and, for the most part, their entrepreneur friends seem harried but happy. So who's to say young women can't be leaders driving the process themselves? Who's to say their companies won't hit it big? As one successful serial entrepreneur put it: "There's only a glass ceiling if you live in the house that's built."

> *These girls aim high. But if they're going to sacrifice sleep and friends and lovers and families, why should it be for "The Man"? Why not have equity, some real skin in the game?*

At the same time, many senior executive women are unmoored by the collapse of a financial system they believed in and helped build. Thirty years ago, they saw themselves as pioneers on the forefront of feminism. They staked their careers and dreams on big companies, and some now feel betrayed. They're sick of reading statistics about the lack of female advancement, sick of celebrating each other at women's conferences that amount to no more than a pat on the back. They can't stomach one more debate on the nuances of "mentor" versus "sponsor." If firms like Lehman Brothers had a few more sisters, they say, maybe we wouldn't be in this mess. From luxury perches in Lake Forest and Greenwich, they're asking: *What have we achieved? Have we come a long way, baby?*

Increasingly, established businesswomen believe the best way to aid subsequent generations is to back female entrepreneurs. These elders may not control who makes partner at Sullivan & Cromwell, but they can marshal their resources to slingshot exceptional female founders to visibility. Looking long term, they know they can still have an impact by investing in self-starters like Shauna Mei.

The Tiger Entrepreneur

Shauna Mei is a rising star who never believed her career would advance through women. She'd recently graduated MIT with a degree in computer science and electrical engineering when she joined Goldman Sachs in 2005 as an analyst in leveraged finance. She figured she'd be competing with the big boys doing semiconductor deals, and initially she wrestled with the staffer who kept placing her, the only female in her group, on fashion deals—or better yet, refinancing tampons and other feminine hygiene products.

Mei didn't want to be pigeonholed by gender, but after a while she learned to use stereotypes to her advantage. While she prided herself on a detailed understanding of tech, in her downtime from work she loved exploring the latest trends. She thought fashion was fun and inspiring, as did many of her brainy girlfriends. And though it might not seem hard-core to male colleagues, she knew there was money to be made here too. Maybe, she thought, she could differentiate herself and earn respect while still pursuing her passions.

Mei told her Goldman bosses she wanted to focus on fashion, and she set out to develop expertise in retail. She handled the sale of Neiman Marcus and worked with private equity firms looking to buy Abercrombie & Fitch. To feed her network, she started attending conferences on her own dime, taking the Delta shuttle from New York up to Harvard to listen to panel discussions. At one such event, Mei found herself absorbed as Jeffry Aronsson, an industry veteran who was CEO of Donna Karan (and before that had been CEO of both Marc Jacobs and Oscar de la Renta), described the luxury market in China, her home country.

> Mei weighed her options. For so many, rising within a pillar firm like Goldman Sachs is the end game, but for her it had always been a stepping-stone.

"He had a very local perspective. Other people were talking numbers and charts, but he took pictures of Chinese girls dressed up in the street," Mei recalls. "He said, '*This* is the real China. They get it, and we need to understand the local culture rather than just look at a fast-growing GDP.'"

When the panel ended and hundreds of people swarmed the stage, Mei turned to exit the auditorium. But suddenly she stopped. "Why not take this opportunity?" she thought, and lingered at the back of the crowd until finally she made eye contact with Aronsson. "Everyone was pushing and shoving cards," Mei says, "but he actually walked over. I said, 'I'd love to get together,' and he said, 'Sure, let's have breakfast.'"

Mei told Aronsson she worked at Goldman, but failed to mention she was a lowly analyst. When Aronsson finally learned this, he was stunned, but by that point they were already doing business. Aronsson wanted to revitalize old brands like London Fog that had vanished because of poor management, and he hoped to buy and oversee a portfolio of companies. So Mei introduced him to higher-ups at Goldman, who considered raising a fund to back Aronsson in his quest. Mei was a twenty-two-year-old cultivating a lucrative client relationship for the firm, and before long she was working on a live deal.

By then, she and Aronsson were talking every day, and when Aronsson decided to quit Donna Karan to found his own firm to do acquisitions and advisory work for luxury brands, he wanted Mei as a partner. Mei weighed her options. For so many, rising within a pillar firm like Goldman Sachs is the end game, but for her it had always been a stepping-stone. "I knew the path, what things would be like at Goldman. I knew how long it took to become partner, even on an accelerated basis," she says. "Through this deal and my networking at Goldman, I had already made several exciting relationships with partners at the firm. I had already found an industry I was passionate about. That's what it was about for me. I didn't know what else I would really get out of it. It was a perfect moment, too good to pass up."

After only fifteen months, Mei left Goldman Sachs to help found The Aronsson Group. She knew her peers thought she was insane. It was close to bonus time and she was walking out with no guarantees.

Both at Goldman and with Aronsson, Mei saw that the luxury fashion space, particularly retail distribution, was controlled by old men. She was shocked by the inefficiencies. It was all about relationships, she says, never about having the right product. Every country was segmented, which made it nearly impossible for talented designers to break out of their home markets to sell internationally.

Take, for example, the Swedish activewear brand Casall. As a fitness junkie, Mei knew the exercise space was dominated by five big brands that catered mostly to men: Nike, Adidas, Reebok, Puma, and Champion. Lululemon and Under Armour had yet to explode on the American scene, and Mei felt there was a sizable market opportunity for a firm that made chic workout clothes for women. She couldn't understand why Casall—which produced the most comfortable, fashionable sports bras and yoga pants—distributed almost exclusively in Scandinavia.

Mei cold-called Casall's founder and CEO and began to develop a relationship, eventually volunteering to go to Sweden for a two- to three-month deep-dive analysis. She was now twenty-five years old, walking into a company with forty employees who had been there on average twenty-five years, in a country she'd never visited. Needless to say, people were suspicious. "I was the youngest person there, I didn't speak Swedish, and I knew the only way I could thrive was to prove to them I could improve the company. I first dove in, had no title, and just got shit done," she says. Mei helped redesign Casall's website, wrote a brand bible translating Swedish into English, set up reporting metrics, and created an internship program—a concept that didn't exist there—with the top Swedish business school.

"They thought I was crazy with my Goldman 100-hour work-weeks, but for me that was normal," she says. "This was something I really believed in."

Aronsson understood that Mei's end goal was to be an operator, so he couldn't have been completely surprised when, three months after she arrived in Sweden, Mei left his firm to become COO of Casall. The C-suite might seem premature for a girl in her twenties, but Mei says Swedes don't focus on titles as much; she and Casall's CEO spent so much time working on efficiency, operations, and execution that "COO" just sounded right. And Mei wore her banner well. She spent a year and a half working side-by-side with the founder, learning how to run a company—sales, distribution, inventory management, import/export.

It was at Casall that Mei had her "aha! moment." She started reviewing the way companies market, and she realized they almost always pursue men. "Only the fashion industry targets women, but we make most purchasing decisions. Apple is the only technology company that knows how to market to women, and look how women drive sales at Apple," she says. "When other industries target women, they market to a woman my mom's age who's in the kitchen wearing an apron. She's frumpy and her hair is in a scrunchie. Who aspires to look like that?"

To Mei, this tactic was ludicrous. At that point she'd spent her career becoming an expert in an industry that exploits the irrational impulse buy, that makes women look at a $3,000 handbag and say, "I gotta have it." And Mei herself is recognizable in chic shift dresses, sporting the latest skull ring or tortoise-shell clutch. How could she channel that same reflex response toward other types of products? Mei wanted to create a socially aware global marketplace to showcase up-and-coming designers and promote sustainable products. She aimed to get women thinking about the impact of their purchases.

"I'm a whole person with 360 degrees of interest, and the only industry marketing to me is fashion?" Mei asks, shaking glossy hair. "Life is so much more than fashion. The objects that we as humans consume drive the livelihood of our world. It's so much more important than markets and billboards. Women could be brand ambassadors. They could change the world by becoming more conscious consumers."

Mei combed the Web and assembled a list of eighty blogs that fed her disparate interests—from fashion to food to technology to travel to philanthropy—but she couldn't find a single website that addressed all these areas simultaneously. Instead, she found herself overwhelmed by a deluge of content. She knew magazines broached these topics, but neither she nor her friends had read print in three years. Plus, she says, these publications don't effectively refresh information online to keep viewers engaged.

> Mei had a mission to change the way products and ideas were launched and to rally women across myriad interests. She saw an opportunity to cater to women, to make online shopping mirror its offline counterpart.

What's more, she thought, online shopping doesn't meet women's needs. The point-and-click approach is undeniably convenient, but Mei believed that in our quest for practicality and efficiency, we'd sacrificed the thrill of discovery. Internet shopping, she says, was designed by men and reflects the way men like to shop. Men go shopping when they need a pair of boxers. They find it in a department store, they buy it, and they leave. But for women, shopping is an exercise in rapture. Women wander into boutiques hoping to be inspired, or they look to trusted advisers to steer them toward products that are special or unique, that they might otherwise never know to search for.

"Girls go shopping as a pastime, not because we're looking for anything in particular. We buy things because our stylish friend recommends them," she says. "I want to re-create that 'aha! moment,' as if you'd stumbled upon something in a street fair or out-of-the-way place. Take something like a handblown glass paperweight from Italy. You don't search for that on the Internet, but when you find it you're inspired by its beauty or craftsmanship."

Mei had a mission to change the way products and ideas were launched and to rally women across myriad interests. She saw an opportunity to cater to women, to make online shopping mirror its offline counterpart. But how could she translate this into a business? Mei began by listing the areas of her life that were important; as a young woman engaged in her world, she wanted to be nourished, enlightened, optimized, dressed, designed, transported, surprised, and treated. With these categories in mind, she set out to design a business that met her own needs, and the needs of vibrant girls just like her.

"I know how to look at natural behaviors and think about how to make them better. And I had the intuition and foresight to know tech would become a natural extension, not an intimidating thing, for women," Mei says. "Businesses that survive will be driven by visionaries. So I entered the industry to learn, and I knew if I allowed myself to learn, I would find something to reinvent. For me it was about how to take this smart, independent, style-conscious woman and feed her bite-size content plus commerce across her entire life."

Living an Aha! Life

From an "aha! moment" a company called AHAlife was born.

Of course, Mei now needed money. She was young, still at the start of her career, and not in a financial position to fund her own firm, and she wanted to see if the concept appealed to those outside her demographic. To test viability, she started reaching out to businesspeople she knew. Her idea was intriguing, they said, but it was Mei's personal story that sealed the deal.

Mei's parents were English professors from China, and they'd left Shauna at home with relatives in 1989 while her father served as a visiting scholar at Brown University. But after the Tiananmen Square massacre occurred, it was deemed unsafe for academics with American ties to return to Beijing. Mei's parents were granted amnesty in the United States, but it would be a year before they were reunited with their treasured only child.

Shauna had been born in Inner Mongolia to a mother who had aborted two previous pregnancies and couldn't bear another loss. She'd ignored doctors' recommendations and carried this girl to term, even after learning her daughter had a heart defect. And in 1990, Shauna arrived in the United States alone, a seven-year-old girl with a hole in her heart.

It would be years before her parents located a surgeon to operate pro bono, and even longer before they found meaningful work. Before settling in Bellevue, Washington, the family lived in Idaho. For a child like Shauna who knew only the glamorous America of old movies, grassy plains blotted by cow dung came as a shock, as did the cramped studio her family shared, shuttling back and forth to a common bathroom down the hall. Mei's father labored as a janitor and at Dairy Queen, while her mother toiled as a maid, dishwasher, baker, and nursing home aide. "In China my parents lived an amazing life, despite the Communists. They had access to everything. But when they moved to the States they had to throw their careers away," Mei says. "I learned everything had implications. I learned life is really short."

Mei started positioning herself for success well before she earned the golden ticket to Goldman Sachs. Her father told her to think about fighting the prevailing notions of Asian women living in America, so she strived to attend a school that would take her outside her boundaries. Though she'd never enjoyed programming, she knew she'd need to understand it to work with techies.

Mei was surrounded by guys in her MIT engineering classes, and when she jumped into banking, she just assumed she'd be working with men. She didn't yearn for "girl power" or even camaraderie among women. "Women didn't really help each other out," she says of Goldman. "You're nice to everyone, but you don't waste your time bonding with other women if you want to get ahead. You try to network with men who are more successful." So it came as a surprise, when Mei launched AHAlife, that Goldman's women became her champions.

Even after she'd moved to Sweden to work for Casall, Mei carried her Goldman network with her. She stayed in touch with people she cared about and could learn from, and she began to contact them about her idea. Mei called Karen Seitz, a former Goldman partner she'd met at a Girl Scouts dinner. Despite their more than twenty-year age difference, the two women clicked. Seitz saw in Mei a kindred spirit who shares her outlook and drive, an intelligent, energetic optimist with great potential.

"In a lot of respects it was a mentorship, but we were friends. Throughout my entire career, all I wanted to do was please and overdeliver and overperform. Shauna has so much of that. She's someone who by this time could be on track to make partner," says Seitz, who now runs her own firm, Fusion Partners, which focuses on alternative investments in areas like private equity, hedge funds, and real estate. "It's exciting to be around people with that kind of conquer-the-world approach to life. And life is long, so I thought maybe there was some potential to do things together, whether on the business or personal front, or giving back."

Mei and Seitz bonded over their 24-7 intensity, their mutual desire to pursue passions rather than find balance. "When people say they want balance, it's because they're looking to turn off when they go home. But there are other people like Shauna and me who always want to integrate work and personal life. If you don't enjoy what you're doing, you shouldn't be doing it," Seitz continues. "For us, the personal and professional are one. If we're satisfied in the work we're doing, it blends into everything we do outside the office, like nonprofits and thinking about the world in a global, macro way. My satisfaction comes from making the world a better place. I'm not an egomaniac, but I think you can have an impact on the world around you on the organizations you care about."

So when Mei came to Seitz with an intention to pursue her company on the side while interviewing for finance jobs, Seitz pushed her to reconsider. "I said, 'Shauna, you have to pursue your dream. This is full-time.' I knew this was a stand-alone," Seitz recalls. "She's very special, and I knew she could do it." Seitz immediately signed on as an investor with $100,000.

Mei also reached out to Janet Hanson, the former Goldman and Lehman Brothers executive who founded 85 Broads, the global professional women's network. Hanson agreed wholeheartedly with Seitz. She threw in $50,000 and introduced Mei to two other Goldman alumnae, Dorothy Price Hill and Sheryl WuDunn, who at the time were both senior managing directors at Mid-Market Securities, a boutique investment bank.

"I heard her story and thought this woman had incredible drive, incredible determination. We were blown away. When you invest in an entrepreneur, you have to know what makes her tick. We really believed in Shauna," says Price Hill, who is now CFO of the TheBarnYardGroup, a media start-up in Stamford, Connecticut.

"People like to invest with people they know, so we spun our platinum Rolodexes. We called everyone who trusted us to tell them about AHAlife."

The women all contributed personally to the $3 million Mei was raising, and they activated their networks. Among others, they introduced Mei to Abigail Disney, the documentary filmmaker and philanthropist, and Lubna Olayan, the CEO of Saudi Arabia–based Olayan Financing Company, the holding entity for her family's multinational empire, who is widely acknowledged as one of the most influential people in the world. They also reached out to a bevy of male colleagues and friends, all of whom took meetings with Mei based on strong referrals.

"Shauna closed every investment after two meetings max. Her investors had either worked with her directly and knew her track record or knew someone who would vouch for her. She had that trust push," Price Hill continues. "If a person I know well shows me an investment, it's a filter. I'll still do my due diligence, but when 80 percent of start-ups fail, the fact that a deal is brought to me by someone I know is very important."

Within three months, Mei's ladies helped rally a list of angel investors that is a who's who of commerce, including John Mack, the former chairman and CEO of Morgan Stanley; Renaud Dutreil, then-chairman of LVMH Moët Hennessy Louis Vuitton North America; the chairman of a top management consulting firm; and the chief executive of another large luxury retail operation. All of whom are men.

In September 2010, Mei launched a media and e-commerce website, AHAlife, with niche products curated by trendsetters and tastemakers she's met through her cadre of influential investors and friends, including Diane von Furstenberg, Tina Brown, Tim Gunn,

Daniel Boulud, and Lauren Bush Lauren. Each day, the site features one new product to furnish some aspect of a global, trendsetting woman's life—from artisanal salami to tribal necklaces, eco-friendly cleaning products, solar-powered lights, portable iPhone speakers, and high-end, high-design vibrators. "Maybe women wouldn't normally search for that on the Internet," she smiles, "but we show you things that make your life better without you asking for it, which is exactly how offline shopping works."

> *Mei is her own target market: a smart, protean girl-about-town who floats easily between fashionistas and MIT geeks.*

AHAlife now has about thirty-five employees, the majority of whom are female, and is projecting annualized 2013 revenue of more than $4 million. The firm opened a physical store in the boutique SLS Hotel in Beverly Hills, raised another $16 million in funding, and strategically partnered with Rakuten, the largest e-commerce site in Japan, which has 75 million consumers.

A quick Google search finds Mei hanging with celebrities like Deepak Chopra and Rachel Roy, and hosting parties with Ivanka Trump and Wendi Murdoch, another Chinese immigrant with whom she's become close. Mei is her own target market: a smart, protean girl-about-town who floats easily between fashionistas and MIT geeks. She's leveraged her tech and business savvy, as well as her Goldman network, and now she will sink or swim on the basis of her vision, her ingenuity, and her ability to execute. Her backers are betting she has the chops.

"She wants to be the Asian Oprah," Sheryl WuDunn says. "She's the Tiger entrepreneur."

Building a Human Pyramid

While Shauna Mei seems remarkable, she is not an outlier. Increasingly, behind aspiring women entrepreneurs stand older female mentors and investors. Many of these elders made it the old way—the hard way, the way with lots of battles—but they're now secure in their positions. Now that there's room for more women at the top, they don't fear being displaced by the younger, newer model. They can breathe. And after forty years of women in the workforce, isn't it easier, not to mention more fun, when "you *or* me" becomes "you *and* me"?

"It's partly because the women in their fifties, having been the only women in the room for a lot of their lives, are exhausted," says Abigail Disney. "The only woman in the room has to act like a man or otherwise she expends all the capital immediately. You weigh and measure every statement. You do a risk assessment every time you open your mouth. You certainly don't want to act like a feminist because that would end it all. It takes a lot out of you to be that person. We always conceived of it as climbing a corporate ladder, but it's more like building a human pyramid, each layer of women supporting the next. Each generation needs the one before."

Disney first met Shauna Mei through Sheryl WuDunn, who is also a documentary filmmaker and, with her husband—the *New York Times* columnist Nicholas Kristof—a Pulitzer Prize winner. When Disney and WuDunn began communicating, it was as competitors. Each was preparing to raise funds for films about women. "Shauna came up at a lunch where we were talking about our projects. I was looking for $4.5 million and [WuDunn] was looking for $2 million, but I wasn't going to elbow my way. We started talking about ways we could work together to raise this money," Disney says. "Maybe it's taken too long to get here from the 1970s, when everyone was looking at cervixes in the mirror. If you don't treat everything as a competition, you get so much more than you lose. We're finally realizing it's much easier to do this together than apart."

Women like Mei's investors are now thinking about legacy. They're keen to give back. But where "giving back" used to mean bestowing advice and a shoulder to cry on, these days it involves access and money too. Now, more than ever, businesswomen are using their self-made wealth to create the world in which they want to live: A world where women build ground-breaking companies that revolutionize industries. A world where women support their families by running innovative businesses. A world where women employ other women and accommodate their needs.

If "even a live wire needs a connection"—as Gordon Macklin, the first president and CEO of NASDAQ, used to say—then senior executive women now provide the connections to young women's live wires by sponsoring and investing in their new ventures. And if they choose wisely, these protégées may be on track to dynastic wealth.

Alexa von Tobel is nothing short of a live wire, and wealth creation is something she thinks women should learn more about. Like Shauna Mei, von Tobel has been a magnet for female support because her mission resonates. She had her "aha! moment" as a Harvard undergrad, after having secured summer internships in consulting and venture capital. Now she'd locked in a job trading derivatives at Morgan Stanley after graduation and she'd be responsible for directing huge sums of other people's money. Yet von Tobel had no idea how to manage her own.

"I wanted to be organized for the future, but I didn't know where to learn anything," she says. "Personal finance isn't taught in schools, yet we make six to ten financial decisions every day." If von

Tobel—an Ivy League woman on Wall Street—knew nothing of personal finance, what were other young ladies doing? How were they going to take care of themselves?

Von Tobel knew Suze Orman was ubiquitous, preaching to women age 45 and over, but who was speaking to her peers? Who was helping smart twenty-somethings stay out of debt in the first place? So von Tobel left Morgan Stanley to enter Harvard Business School and, like any good student, started doing her homework. She spent a year researching women's finance and began cornering every professor who would listen. When enough of them said, "Kid, you're onto something," she made her move.

Von Tobel dropped out of Harvard and, eighty-page business plan in hand, moved to New York to raise money. It was January 2009, and the recession was fully under way. Bernie Madoff's Ponzi scheme had drained deep pockets, and Lehman Brothers was bankrupt. Though it would be three years before Greg Smith wrote his lacerating *New York Times* op-ed piece decrying Goldman's "toxic and destructive" ethos, and even longer before the "London Whale" blew a $6.2 billion hole in JPMorgan, no one believed bankers were doing "God's work." Against this backdrop, Park Avenue matrons were hiding shopping bags from Wall Street husbands at higher-than-average rates. Trust was very low.

Von Tobel began making calls, and she consigned her entire post-college savings—tens of thousands of dollars—to her venture so potential investors would know she was 100 percent committed. "I didn't want to take money from friends and family," she says. "I wanted to take money from people who could move my business a mile forward." Soon, it seemed, all roads led to Ann Kaplan.

Kaplan had been a pre-IPO partner in the municipal bond department at Goldman Sachs and now sits on the board of Goldman Sachs

Bank USA. She taught asset and wealth management at Columbia Business School and had founded the Center for Women's Financial Independence at her alma mater, Smith College. And in 2003, Kaplan established Circle Financial Group, which began as an investment think tank for high-net-worth women in finance, many of whom had been partners at Goldman and Morgan Stanley. Circle Financial members work together to provide access to investment opportunities and offer financial education to women who've been successful in other fields. No one was more passionate than Ann Kaplan about female financial literacy.

Though she rarely angel-invests, Kaplan was an expert in von Tobel's space, and she knew this young woman's thesis was right. "Alexa was using what we already knew to be true. We thought it was important to get the message out to younger women that if they run their investments as a business . . . they can make money on their money," she says. "Alexa's mission was totally synergistic with my mission and with the other members of Circle Financial." And she thought von Tobel's energy, commitment, self-confidence, and vision were extraordinary in a woman her age. Ann Kaplan has children older than her protégée, but she was ready to bet on both the company and on Alexa von Tobel.

> *"This is not just a financial relationship. It's one of passion, true loyalty, care, and concern for our mission. These incredible women have rolled up their sleeves and been involved in the nitty-gritty of building my business." —Alexa von Tobel*

Kaplan and two other members of Circle Financial—Jacki Zehner and Maria Chrin—provided hundreds of thousands of dollars of seed funding for von Tobel's company, LearnVest, and helped von

Tobel woo additional investors, both male and female. Within six months, in the heat of a recession, von Tobel wrangled $1.1 million.

LearnVest's backers haven't stopped at money; they've also spent time and energy helping von Tobel succeed. Kaplan gave von Tobel access to Circle Financial's research and wrote content for the site. She's hosted weekend strategy sessions in her home for the LearnVest team, as well as cocktail parties to introduce investors and interested parties to von Tobel. Zehner presented von Tobel to Janet Riccio, an executive vice president at Omnicom Group, who became a formal adviser to help build LearnVest's brand. The ladies all sit together at events like TEDWomen, and they shepherd von Tobel around to make sure everyone knows she's a player.

"This is not just a financial relationship. It's one of passion, true loyalty, care, and concern for our mission. These incredible women have rolled up their sleeves and been involved in the nitty-gritty of building my business," von Tobel says. "I'm from a tiny town in Florida. No one in my family went to Harvard, and it's not like I fell off a truck with $1 million in my pocket. I've worked incredibly hard and I've watched women bend over backwards to open doors for me. This was all about people who are connected to other people."

Von Tobel officially opened LearnVest's doors in December 2009, and by January 2010, she knew she'd struck a chord. Some 10,000 subscribers signed on within the first few days, and von Tobel fed off their gusto, as hundreds of users e-mailed to say they'd been looking for just this service. Venture capitalists came knocking, and von Tobel found herself flying to meetings in Boston and on the West Coast. In a flurry of term sheets, she chose to work with Theresia Gouw Ranzetta, the only female partner in the United States at Accel Partners, which is based in Silicon Valley. Accel invested $4.5 million in LearnVest, and von Tobel added another high-octane gal to her A-team.

LearnVest has since raised another $19 million from Accel and other investors. The company has about sixty-five employees, two-thirds of whom are female, and some 500,000 users. Von Tobel and her staff work with experts to create free interactive content and tools, and they make money through advertising and premium services. LearnVest recently became a registered investment adviser with a call center of certified financial planners, to whom users pay $350 for a five-year financial plan. Von Tobel describes these developments as "Apple's Genius Bar meets personal finance," and ultimately hopes to give institutions like Merrill Edge and Bank of America a run for their money.

LearnVest is positioning itself as a hybrid-media company, and von Tobel herself has become quite the media darling. She's been featured in scores of magazines, newspapers, and TV programs. She was named on *Vanity Fair's* 2011 "Next Establishment" list; on *Business Insider's* Silicon Alley 100 lists of New York's "coolest tech people" in 2010, 2011, and 2012; on *Inc.* magazine's list of "30 Under 30: Top Young Entrepreneurs" of 2010; as a "Woman to Watch" by *Forbes*; as one of the 2011 "Best Young Tech Entrepreneurs" by *BusinessWeek*; and as one of "18 Women Changing the World" by *Marie Claire* in 2010. She was also selected as a 2011 Young Global Leader by the World Economic Forum and has been a speaker at the South by Southwest (SXSW) conference and top business schools. In October 2010, she spoke at Maria Shriver's "Women's Conference" in California. This girl is everywhere.

Like Shauna Mei, von Tobel has used her personal insights to create a business aimed at her peers. Like Mei, she found people—women—who could intimately understand and relate to her concept. And like Mei, von Tobel represents the brand. She's a sweet and charming girls' girl who tosses long hair, coos over a sparkly engagement ring, and swoons while recounting how her fiancé proposed. A little blond thunderclap, she bursts with enthusiasm and smiles contagiously through rapid-fire patter. Her coiled energy leaves others breathless.

Had she been born forty years earlier, von Tobel might have had to look and act like a man to succeed in finance. But today her appeal to women paves her way. Her very girliness may send her laughing all the way to the bank.

The Ultimate Exit Strategy

Young women like Mei and von Tobel are reaping the benefits of senior executives' cumulative wealth and experience, but it's not only the upstarts who profit when their elders co-invest. Executive women's horizontal networks are becoming ever more robust. Just as a child strengthens the bond of marriage, financial ties add another dimension to friendships.

"My relationship with Sheryl [WuDunn] is stronger, and it was so nice that Janet Hanson was involved because I knew her years ago. When someone crops back up, it's a sign you're in the right place. I could see where it could go terribly wrong, but for us it's been positive," says Abigail Disney, who seldom angel-invests but says she didn't do a lot of digging because Shauna Mei's AHAlife had come "preapproved" by WuDunn. "We all have that much more in common now and we're rooting for the same thing. Women have to get a little less afraid to talk about money together. We need to be less apologetic about money and power."

Because these women have long been major players on a field full of men, they never considered working in isolation. Of course, they've brought guys along for the ride, and as a result their relationships with male colleagues have improved too. As Dorothy Price Hill, who is in her mid-forties, puts it, "We can't sit in the corner complaining about the world and burning our bras, and we can't do these things in a vacuum. We have to be at the table with men, creating solutions." One solution is to be indispensable, to become a source for deals that make investors millions, if not billions. If AHAlife succeeds, Mei's angel investors will see a handsome return on their money. In many cases, it was women who showcased AHAlife and provided the connective tissue, so the boys will have the girls to thank.

> "We can't sit in the corner complaining about the world and burning our bras, and we can't do these things in a vacuum. We have to be at the table with men, creating solutions." —Dorothy Price Hill

In the meantime, Mei's investors are seeing returns of a different sort. "Shauna has put together an impressive group of investors. Being part of it is valuable for me and my business," says Scott Prince, a real estate investor and former Goldman partner who invested personal money in AHAlife. Prince met Mei through her mentor and friend, Karen Seitz, and now he's benefiting in ways he didn't predict. "I've met people who may not have been in my inner circle before and can now expand my contacts even further."

And it's not just Prince who's found ancillary value by associating with Mei. Mei says Renaud Dutreil (who was a highly ranked French government minister before he joined LVMH) told her he'd never miss one of her investor dinners because they provide such great networking for him. He recently collaborated on a luxury leather goods company with another AHAlife backer, and two more AHAlife investors are considering a joint venture in Indonesia—all because they all connected through Shauna Mei.

Now, with the help of some "platinum Rolodexes," Mei finds herself, at just 30, a hub with many male sovereigns as spokes on her wheel. Suddenly, instead of Mei capitalizing on their influence, they're leveraging hers. Each of Mei's investors contributed $250,000 or less—mere play money to these honchos—but they're forming compelling personal alliances worth far more than the cash.

So the question becomes: Would Mei be at the center of this power structure if she'd stayed at Goldman, or slogged away at any big firm?

"What's interesting is that most of us with money to invest grew up in the world of banking or finance, but if we could we'd come back in the next life as Alexa or Shauna," Janet Hanson says emphatically, pounding the table as she did on Wall Street. "It's fascinating to see how Shauna got the joke that some of the biggest fashion retailers are run by men. It's mind-blowing how clearly she saw the trade at Goldman. Was Shauna likely to get promoted so quickly? Probably not. But she stepped out of Goldman and took their money.

"Men still control most of the institutional dollars," Hanson continues, "so how do you ensure women get the highest possible return on their education? If you're lucky enough to be at a firm like Goldman Sachs, you work your network up. You come up with your idea and start lining up investors while you're there. The combined net worth of partners at Goldman is in the billions, and Shauna understood how to use that opportunity to her advantage. Shauna's not the first female who thought, 'This might work out, but if I look at it from a different angle, holy shit. I can do more. I can make this network work for me.' That's the ultimate exit strategy."

"GIRLPRENEURS" RISING

Many established women invest in young ladies' start-ups thinking they'll bestow wisdom and shape a career. But almost without fail, they end up expounding on what they've gained in return. A few years ago, Nancy Peretsman, the eminent investment banker at Allen & Company—who has served the likes of Oprah Winfrey, Rupert Murdoch, and Google's executive chairman, Eric Schmidt—started inviting both female entrepreneurs and corporate moguls to her company's ranch in Cody, Wyoming, and to Sun Valley, Idaho, the site of Allen & Company's renowned annual conference, where Mark Zuckerberg rubs elbows with Bill Gates.

Peretsman keeps her groups small and intimate, no more than a dozen women who leave their day jobs behind to talk about improving both businesses and personal lives. "It was the biggest hit! And we had a couple of real eye-openers," she says. "We thought the younger women would deeply benefit from the older women, but the surprise was that it definitely went both ways."

The elders talk about risk taking and share detailed knowledge to help the younger gals get a leg up. "To have a senior money manager say to CEOs of public companies, 'Guys, let me tell you how it really works when we look at an IPO. In this cone of silence, I'll tell you how my world works so when somebody says something you'll know what it means.' That's valuable, raw information that would be very difficult to get otherwise."

The entrepreneurs bring a deep knowledge of technology. In one instance, when a techie learned that a senior media executive was planning to use a particular platform, she balked and immediately offered to help find the right alternative.

"There's no macro plan or Machiavellian intention. You never really know where the help comes from," says Peretsman, who has also personally invested in young women's ventures. "The women in their thirties have all the same questions: Should we go out on our own? How to manage life, family, career? And the older women were thrilled by the energy and enthusiasm they brought to bear. In some cases it's an attempt to help, to make the right introductions. And in other cases it's: Can we give her money?"

Cultivating a New Crop

Susan Lyne, the chairman and former CEO of Gilt Groupe, a flash-sale site valued in 2011 at $1 billion, has attended Peretsman's events and has also profited from mentoring young women. Lyne says that for the past ten years, she has met with at least two gals per week who are somehow referred to her. She keeps it short, never more than thirty minutes, and gets straight to the point: What should this woman know to move forward? Whom can Lyne connect her with? How can she help?

"The longer you're working, the more you realize how things like that pay back a thousandfold. I hear so often from someone from Spencer Stuart, or another recruiting firm checking on me, that they heard something nice about me. Sometimes I don't even remember the person who said it," says Lyne, who is slim, blond, and radiant in her early sixties. "Why do it? Part is legacy, but part is self-interest. The broader your reach over time, the greater the benefit for you."

Lyne had an impressive career in "old media" companies when she decided to jump ship for a start-up, and she says her willingness to mentor helped land her current gig. She was the president and CEO of Martha Stewart Living Omnimedia, and before that spent eight years at the Walt Disney Company and ABC, rising to president of ABC Entertainment. Prior to that, she'd logged fifteen years in magazines. But she signed on as CEO of Gilt Groupe in 2008, less than a year after the company's launch, and has grown her firm to 900 employees, more than 3 million subscribers, and six different business lines in the United States. The company is considering going public in 2013.

To make this jump, Lyne needed faith in Kevin Ryan, Gilt's founder and a flourishing serial entrepreneur, and she also had to be in sync with Alexandra Wilkis Wilson and Alexis Maybank, the young Harvard MBAs who cofounded Gilt Groupe and were chosen as the face of the brand. "Alexandra is laser-focused on brand relationships. She starts the day with a list and doesn't end until she's crossed everything off. Alexis is strategic, thoughtful, and will have a very serious leadership career. She really is a rising star," Lyne says of her colleagues. "It's fun to work with these women who, if you look at the age gap, could really be my daughters."

> *Some of today's greatest opportunities stem from unproven sources, be they twenty-two-year-old college dropouts or women who've ditched corporate life or taken a break to raise children.*

More and more, female senior executives are teaming up with Gen Y and Millennials to launch and lead new ventures, providing the management expertise and "adult supervision" start-ups need to steer the course. Experienced women like Lyne now find themselves idealistically aligned with a younger generation. They are open to partnering with today's youth—twenty-somethings who crave flexibility and control, who have historically taken a back seat and now want their voices heard.

Some of today's greatest opportunities stem from unproven sources, be they twenty-two-year-old college dropouts or women who've ditched corporate life or taken a break to raise children. If women are receptive to these alliances, they'll be more likely to capitalize on their success. It's a risk, but one that's paying off for gals like Sheryl Sandberg, the COO of Facebook, who took a chance on Mark Zuckerberg. Or Lyne, who says that when she was being considered for the top job at Gilt Groupe, the firm's investors and management cast a wide net to get feedback on her. "It confirms what I've said. It benefited me enormously that I've given a little time to people at crucial moments in their careers," she says. "Talented people will always reconnect with you."

Only recently have women learned the power of cultivating the next generation, something men have long known. "One thing the Old Boys' Network understood was that it wasn't always about people at your level. They understood the important thing was to bring the next generation along," says Edie Weiner, one of the nation's leading futurists and president of Weiner, Edrich, Brown, Inc. "It's the Godfather principle. It strengthens your business networks if you hire the sons of your friends. When these guys aged out or retired, the next generation was there for them too."

From the armed forces to labor unions to the white-collar elite, men at the top have exploited subsequent generations to secure their own authority and relevance. If their acolytes felt grateful and indebted, they wouldn't cast aside mentors past their prime. By reaching down and pulling up, the Old Guard stayed vital and engaged well into their sunset years.

"We're living longer and women are realizing if all you care about is knowing women at your level, you retire and then what? If you want some consulting engagements or to volunteer, you'd better realize it's going to be for an organization run by a thirty-five-year-old," Weiner continues. "If all you want to do is rise and then retire at age 65, then maybe you can care only about the women your own age and level. But if you want to remain vibrant until you're 85, you'd better have a connection to younger generations."

Lady Business

Now, unlike in generations past, instead of just receiving help, women in their twenties and thirties are extending a hand to their peers. As if taking a cue from executive elders, female entrepreneurs like Shauna Mei, Alexa von Tobel, Alexis Maybank, and Alexandra Wilkis Wilson are also furiously networking with other women. Just like the ladies of The Vault and 4C2B, women founders have a shared set of experiences. They talk nonstop about business. And while their companies span the industries—from finance to real estate to fashion to art—they're almost all Web-based. As a result, young female CEOs have become each other's strategic advisers.

But it's not like they're all work and no play. These chicks are a bundle of contradictions, and they're cool with that. They're clever and giddy, cocky and scared, tough and treacly, in and out of touch. They aspire to be in the *New York Times*, but many don't read it. They bookmark HuffPo and BuzzFeed, snark with Jon Stewart, and guffaw with Tina Fey. They're sour on Wall Street, but desperate for a date to the Robin Hood gala. They know Marissa Mayer clinched a sweet deal at Yahoo and they know she was preggers, but whatever. Let the pundits feast.

They've read that Kim Kardashian bought panties at Journelle, but couldn't spot Clare Boothe Luce in a lineup. They grieve the loss of Nora Ephron and lament that the brainy-sexy rebellion of Dorothy Parker and Mary McCarthy has yielded to catfights on *Mob Wives* and *Teen Mom*. But they quote *Jersey Shore*, that bleating of busty dingbats in cutoffs. They turn up their noses at *Real Housewives*, but esteem Bethenny Frankel's branded franchise. What's her Klout Score, anyway?

These ladies go high and low, unfazed by antipodes, vacillating between flatlining dross and intellectual pyrotechnics. The same girls who devoured geopolitics and deconstructed Derrida in college, who toss off words like *syllogism* and *simulacrum*, who've at least heard of the Higgs boson? They still sing all the words to "Call Me Maybe." And when Karmin raps "business in the front, party in the back," they know that band's not defining the mullet. These are wise words for life. It'll be years before they learn that miscarriages are like Botox— everyone's done it at least once—but when the time comes, they won't stand on ceremony. The dermatologist is their friend.

They're whipped into a collective lather over *Girls*, mounting the media's erection for Lena Dunham, glued to her self-flagellation because it's part of their journey too. And like Dunham's character, Hannah, they're leaning on girlfriends. Even a cohort that embraces random hookups and drinks Big Gulps of irony wants something to care about, something to matter. These young women might not admit it, but they want to be the voice of their generation too. They aspire to greatness. Ride, Sally Ride.

> *"We're living in this exciting time where we can feel innovation all around us. It's fun to have drinks and talk girl stuff, and it's also impressive that there are so many women launching high-growth businesses"—Alexa von Tobel*

So what if they don't have all the answers? They're not trying to reconcile Bella Abzug and Gloria Steinem with Naomi Wolf and Camille Paglia. Seriously. They're too busy working. Never has the Women's Movement felt less like a jaundiced faction and more like a party. Female entrepreneurs are having a rollicking good time.

Just watch the action at Lady Business, a series of girl fêtes hosted by a group that includes Alexa von Tobel and Alexa Hirschfeld, the cofounder of Paperless Post, a purveyor of fine stationery via e-mail. Liquor is flowing and pizza is delivered as more than 100 gals between ages 24 and 40 rock until 3 AM. They've scurried downtown to Hirschfeld's East Village apartment, and they're talking to strangers, trading business cards, and promising to follow up. There's electricity here, like at a political rally or protest. It's a hothouse, a pot ready to boil.

"We're living in this exciting time where we can feel innovation all around us. It's fun to have drinks and talk girl stuff, and it's also impressive that there are so many women launching high-growth businesses, much more than even a year ago," von Tobel says with characteristic urgency. "People aren't being fake. We're in this recession and everyone's a little worried, so this group is banding together and being 100 percent supportive. So let's learn about each other's products. Let's help each other get funding. It's not that we can't get guys together, but we're starting to feel there's a community of women."

Shauna Mei hasn't reveled at Lady Business, but she's surrounded by her own clique of tech-girls she met a few years ago on a four-day trip to the "Founders Conference" in Dublin (an annual gathering of tech entrepreneurs). "It was 95 percent men and we [the women] really bonded as a result. We've been spending a lot of time hanging out and it's proved really helpful," she says. Because AHAlife features culinary items among its wares, Mei and Soraya Darabi, the cofounder of the Internet food guide Foodspotting, sponsored a food-themed event to introduce their supporters and investors. And Mei's other pals—including Amy Sacco, the nightlife and branding maven—have all opened doors. "I chat with these girls through social media almost daily," Mei continues. "We probably see each other at least once a month, and we're constantly talking about business and funding and considering strategic collaborations."

Mei, Darabi, and von Tobel are also regulars at Calliope Group breakfasts, where gaggles of girls sport platform heels and designer dresses while nibbling egg-white wraps at tables draped in hot pink. Who needs flowers when there's this much perfume? Their panache is an affront to stereotypical techies, or like a dream sequence from *Revenge of the Nerds*. But make no mistake: This is a room full of geeks. The Calliope ladies are mostly in their twenties and thirties, and they've launched what they hope will be high-growth online companies. They too are turning to their peers to exchange funding tips, run their businesses, and ultimately create wealth.

"These women are now friends. We all hang out and support each other and recommend each other for panels," says Dina Kaplan, cofounder of Blip, a site that features original Web video, and Calliope Group's organizer. "It's a very serious, solid base from which business deals are forming."

And who else is milling around? Women of a certain age. Susan Lyne and the Internet pioneer Esther Dyson. Not to mention Pat Mitchell, president and CEO of the Paley Center for Media, and Wenda Harris Millard, the Yahoo veteran and president of MediaLink.

So the older gals all know each other, and now the younger gals all know each other. Suddenly, these two groups are coming together and money is changing hands. "This seems counterintuitive because we all think we have these proprietary ideas," Susan Lyne says. "But any time there's been the equivalent of an 'Arab spring' in some industry, it's because people are communicating and sharing." That's exactly what's happening here. Rising female entrepreneurs are the spark that has ignited their elders, fueling a networking and funding trend that is top-down, bottom-up, and intergenerational.

This grassroots eruption, which has clusters on the coasts and offshoots far beyond, is a testament to what Sara Holoubek—the founder and CEO of Luminary Labs, a management consulting firm—identifies as an "underground railroad" or series of coordinated efforts to raise the profile of women leaders. In fall 2010, partly in response to the persistent dearth of women on *Business Insider*'s Silicon Alley list of New York's 100 "Coolest Tech People," Holoubek canvassed her colleagues and friends to list the smartest, most capable women they knew. She then published *A Field Guide to the Female Founders, Influencers and Deal Makers of NYC* and invited ladies on the list to her Tribeca duplex to share ideas. Though the *Field Guide* crowd skews older than Calliope Group—you see a few wrinkles here, and participants favor wine and Holoubek's home-made Middle Eastern spread over beer and pizza—its goals are the same: building companies and making money.

"It's not agenda-based. It's someone saying, 'You need to meet this person,' and that person happens to be another talented woman," Holoubek says. "Then as people are looking for speakers, or to hire someone or do a deal, women come to mind because they're already in the network."

The Wafia

Holoubek was also front and center at Women Entrepreneurs Poker Night, an event at Heidi Messer's Tribeca high-rise in June 2011. This group, which included a smattering of *Field Guide* gals and a multitude of others, was billed as another "grown-up" addition to women's mixers that have been proliferating. Messer, who is in her early forties, had cleared furniture from her living room and pitched long tables covered in green felt. She greeted guests before ducking down a hallway to tuck her young children in bed, while her cohosts—fellow entrepreneurs and angel investors—invited ladies to partake of catered sushi and fillet. Poker chips were stacked in neat bundles, and customized cheat sheets showed a woman's hands tipped by vampy red nails, holding the aces.

Messer emerged and began chatting amiably with women who want to be her, who know that in the mid-1990s, Messer and her brother devised a system to monetize advertising on the Internet. They spent ten years building LinkShare, running offices across the United States and in Europe and Japan before selling the company in 2005 for $425 million. Messer briefly tried retirement, which she doesn't recommend for anyone in her thirties. "I got bored really fast. I got married, had two kids, and started another business in the past five years," she says. "I just had a baby four months ago, so I'm always looking to talk to women who've done it."

> "How do I do it? I'm financially secure. I have that advantage, so I've hired the village. Every successful woman has people behind her."—Heidi Messer

Now the siblings are back at it, having founded another firm with Messer's husband, the former COO of Overstock.com. Messer says she works ridiculously hard as an entrepreneur, but she also has total flexibility. Her two partners understand the requirements of their business, and they also appreciate each other's personal needs; they collaborate to make sure everyone feels fulfilled. "I have an unbelievably supportive husband. Every successful woman has a supportive husband, respecting where she's coming from, making compromises and sacrifices," Messer says. "Then I have my very supportive brother who isn't going to question if I have to go to the pediatrician in the afternoon."

And, to call a spade a spade—they're playing cards, after all—money makes life easier. "How do I do it? I'm financially secure. I have that advantage, so I've hired the village. Every successful woman has people behind her," she continues straightforwardly. "My mom is also unbelievably helpful and she feels it's very important that I work and my daughter sees that as normal."

This time around, Messer says other ladies "who've done it" are easy to find. Unlike a decade ago, she's suddenly surrounded by a "Wafia," or Women's Mafia, that didn't exist before. "For the first time we're seeing women really going for it, not sitting around and saying 'Woe is me,' but saying 'Who do you know? How can I get ahead?'" she says. "These women are getting funding and exposure, helping each other succeed."

What stokes allegiances better than poker? Someone recently told Messer that "poker is the new golf"; it takes a few hours and is useful for business strategy, with all the bonus of the "smoky room" and none of the coughing. So she's drawing on her broad network to assemble a regular group to play.

Messer is at the core of a booming entrepreneurial scene in New York. She knows the venture capitalists in town, and she regularly feeds them tips and vets new founders. And because she had a financial bonanza at a young age, she's in a position to angel-invest earlier than most. She's always thinking of smart ways to put her money to work, so part of the point of Poker Night is to get gifted female entrepreneurs mingling with VCs. Now they're all in the same room, talking smack over cards.

"I think this group of women coming up is the smartest. They're so observant," Messer says. "They've figured out things it took me years to figure out. They're doing it so flawlessly. They're not having parades about it; they're just executing."

The young ladies Messer describes have listened to their corporate elders, women who say—in whispers, behind closed doors—that you can have everything, just not all at once. Or at least they admit it's really damn hard. Perhaps Wafia girls have seen their mothers and sisters stressed and strung out, never feeling good enough. For Millennials, success seems a Pyrrhic victory once they've read Anne-Marie Slaughter's 2012 *Atlantic* piece on *not* "having it all." Or watched female bosses bashing bumbling husbands who can't manage to make dinner, much less load the dishwasher (*Doesn't he know*

I work too?). Or cursing face time like Kryptonite, a yoke around their necks. Or fretting on UrbanBaby.com. Or pretending to listen on conference calls while lining up tutors for their kids, making stupid mistakes because they're pulled in so many directions they can't do anything well. Or pumping themselves full of hormones, then retreating to their offices to cry, having explained to a six-year-old niece that no, the Easter Bunny can't harvest eggs.

Some portal to the future.

Women in their twenties are keen observers. They know their elders talk a good game about balance, then fall into bed in a heap. These old broads might not wear aprons and scrunchies, but they look like they haven't slept in years. *This* is living the dream? Who do they think they're fooling? No wonder they're sleeping with *Fifty Shades of Grey.*

Instead, "girlpreneurs" aim to take it one step at a time. They'll pull out all the stops now to make a pile of dough, if only to buy themselves choices. Given the alternatives, who wouldn't rather be Heidi Messer?

> *Young female founders are playing offense rather than defense. It feels like now or never.*

"Women today don't necessarily think of themselves in forty-year careers. They know they have the opportunity to prove themselves before they have kids, so it's more intense," Alexa Hirschfeld says. "Working at Goldman Sachs on a forty-year career schedule doesn't work. Entrepreneurship does. So women are capitalizing on something broken in the system. They're rushing in. It's like a land grab. Why would you go into an established industry when you can enter one growing at an astronomical rate?"

For wannabe Messers, it's go-go-go. Young female founders are playing offense rather than defense. They're raising each other's profiles. They're promoting each other's businesses. They're all one degree of separation and they fly coast-to-coast to attend each other's events. There's a duplication of names in these groups because women are no longer confined to one sphere. They have multiple networks that are fast converging. It feels like now or never.

And while it wasn't their plan, female entrepreneurs have begun to replace Wall Street as a job creation engine for recent college grads. Lots of sharp kids are struggling to find work in the recession. Traditional suitors like consulting firms and banks aren't courting—and, as mentioned, college students who've seen their parents suffer in the financial crisis now disdain the establishment. Law school seems like another dead end. Large media companies might be hiring, but they don't necessarily come to campus, and neither do start-ups hunting for a few key employees.

Not to mention that on-campus recruiting is just short of ante-diluvian. Career Services budgets have been slashed as college endowments dwindle. Besides, even in boom years, most offices yielded little more than event calendars. Counselors aren't tapped into "new economy" jobs.

At the same time, our 24-7 work culture all but ensures that mentoring and hiring will never again occur at random. The graying statesmen who thirty years ago might have struck up con-versations with youngsters on trains are now engrossed in their smartphones. These days they're popping Viagra and dyeing their hair, trying to preserve their own youth rather than shine a light on some whippersnapper.

And here's another issue: Social networking, so all-consuming to the nation's twenty-somethings, is not going to get them hired.

Facebook status updates on your Pilates workout won't help land a job, but posting pictures of yourself doing body shots in a bra can certainly hinder a search. "How do you *lime* me now?" one *chiquita* smolders. So far, the dangers outweigh the upside. Millennials are networking, but it's not quite strategic.

Helicopter parents think they can loosen the reins once offspring surface with fancy degrees, but their problems are just beginning. The Pew Research Center estimates that more than one-third of eighteen- to twenty-nine-year-olds are unemployed or out of the workforce, the highest percentage in more than thirty years. In 2011, nearly 54 percent of people under age 25 with bachelor's degrees were jobless or underemployed, the most in eleven years, according to the Center for Labor Market Studies at Northeastern University. No one is guiding precious progeny toward some professional Valhalla. Unless these kids figure out how to network to create options, they're moving home.

"The real bubble of being at Princeton or wherever is that you're surrounded by people who are brilliant. The big firms used to absorb enough smart kids and re-create that atmosphere," says Janet Hanson of 85 Broads. "But nowadays, most kids are going to get out of college and wander for two or three years. Then they take whatever job they can get and their fire goes out. They attribute it to not liking their jobs, but the truth is their intellects are not stimulated in a way that fires up their creativity. We need a better recruiting system so these kids can lever up their massive intellects and retain that passion. If you can make the right connections earlier on, it can change your life big-time."

How does the "entitlement generation" sidestep stultifying malaise, that compounding sense of dislocation? How do they find jobs that keep them fired up? By staying in touch with friends who left school just a few years before, by joining their companies, by feeling they're all in this mosh pit together, and maybe—just maybe—changing the world. Of course, they won't all succeed. Most will fail miserably. But they'll fail in seminar-like atmospheres that fuel their ambition and drive, and they'll want to keep trying, again and again, until they stand as equals with Heidi Messer.

For ladies launching companies, this means networking down and cultivating younger women even earlier than Edie Weiner suggested. Female entrepreneurs aren't waiting decades to hire and mentor; they're fast-forwarding the process so it feels more like cloning than spawning. It's the modern manifestation of that classic Fabergé shampoo commercial: "It was so good that I told two friends about it, and they told two friends, and so on and so on and so on . . . ."

They've spent less than ten years in the workforce, but already they're traveling back to alma maters to poach top talent. They're grabbing girls the banks and consulting firms are missing, girls who in another era would have lobbied to join the Wall Street fraternity. But now they're rushing this new media sorority, as Lady Business, Calliope Group, *Field Guide*, and Poker Night welcome them with open arms.

The Big (Girl) Bang

There's been a Big (Girl) Bang, and constellations of energized young ladies have alighted on the scene. Venture capitalists say they've seen a huge influx of female entrepreneurs in the last five years, and many think it's the start of a virtuous circle. "More women entrepreneurs will lead to more women executives," says Theresia Gouw Ranzetta, the Accel partner who is on *Forbes*'s Midas List of Top Tech Investors. "Women who create their own companies are more likely to rise more quickly in the world, and they set the tone for their companies' cultures and promotion systems." In short, women hire and promote more women. More women at the top lead to more women rising in the ranks.

Alexa Hirschfeld goes a step further, saying that hiring women has become a core business strategy for her company, Paperless Post. She believes women are still discriminated against in technology, and she's more than happy to capitalize on this market inefficiency to build her firm. "I've never seen the world through a gender lens. I was never a girly girl and I didn't like feminism. I just believe in being good at what I do," she says. "So for us it's not an HR thing. We're trying to get the best people to build the best company, and I've hired more senior employees than I would have otherwise been able to get because they were women." She references one female employee with a computer science background who sold her earlier company to the Japanese Amazon.com, and a database and analytics engineer who's a leader in the women's tech community.

The difference between a $100 million company and a $1 billion company is the team. Bosses always hire by proxy; men think rock-star developers are dudes with shaggy hair who live in Brooklyn, chug Mountain Dew, and carry MacBooks. "But if you're a woman, you realize there are actually girls out there with the same or better skills. If you can recognize talent in a person who doesn't look like the normal candidate, you can get someone even more qualified because she appreciates that you appreciate her," continues Hirschfeld, who is in her late twenties. "The women here are the alpha people. We are ambitious and we have a better team because we have no gender biases. It's an edge we're capitalizing on for selfish reasons, not political reasons."

These tactics have led to success and growth, as Paperless Post becomes a household name. Revenues doubled from 2010 to 2011 and are expected to nearly triple between 2011 and 2012. Hirschfeld anticipates her company will be profitable by 2013. Her strategy has also bred an environment defined by trust for fifty employees, half of whom are female. "It's informal, honest, social, and warm," she says. "People genuinely like each other, and we're always thinking about what's best for the business."

What's best for business is now hanging out with other ladies. Paperless Post's users are 75 to 80 percent female, so Hirschfeld believes it's important to have women listening and creating products that appeal to their friends. "People here are light-years ahead of people I'd be socializing with otherwise," Hirschfeld says of the Calliope Group breakfasts. "I'm meeting the chairman of Gilt, the founder of One Kings Lane [a home decor website], people on the management team of AOL. I really like them, and it's opportunistic. It's all about access."

As a result, female entrepreneurs' informal interactions function as de facto business incubators, and money is flowing their way. Venture capitalists are beginning to tap into these networks as they realize that the entrepreneurs they fund can sniff out new talent and source their next big deal. For one, Alexa von Tobel introduced Theresia Gouw Ranzetta to two close girlfriends—the twenty-something entrepreneurs behind Birchbox, a cosmetics enterprise, and BaubleBar, a jewelry company. Accel Partners then funded these firms.

Accel recently opened a New York office to manage its investments there, about one-quarter of which include a female founder on the team. This is high, Ranzetta says, given that only about 10 percent of venture-backed companies nationwide have women founders or chief executives. "Last fall, I had a dinner in New York for all of my portfolio companies," she says. "It happened to be ten women and me."

Venture capitalists also say the pipeline for female entrepreneurs has been growing because technology has become cheaper and easier to replicate. Less capital is required to start a business, which lowers the bar for all entrepreneurs. Today's technology companies are Web-based but not necessarily rooted in proprietary tools like semiconductors. All sorts of businesses have migrated online, and entrepreneurs no longer need computer science degrees—where women have historically lagged—to launch viable concerns.

"When I started out in venture, it was about technology—boxes, bits, bites, hard-core techie stuff. You rarely saw women engineers, which is why women in tech have been so underrepresented," says Lawrence Lenihan, Jr., the founder and managing director of FirstMark Capital, a venture capital firm based in New York. "But in the last five years, you have companies being built on this incredible tech infrastructure. You have to be strong in tech, but you don't have to be a coder. What you really have to understand is the industries."

Female entrepreneurs may not all be powerhouse mathematicians, programmers, or designers, but many have learned enough JavaScript, Ruby on Rails, and HTML to manage and communicate with their tech teams. Moreover, these gals are serious, shrewd businesspeople with insight into their industries. A quick survey of companies thriving today—take Facebook, YouTube, LinkedIn, Twitter, Pinterest, Gilt Groupe, and Zynga—shows they're concepts regular people (i.e., non-geeks) comprehend, and women have a natural affinity for the ideas. As more active users of this technology, they're in an ideal position to recognize market opportunities.

Lenihan points to retail as an obvious example of a business women know intimately and a silo ripe for disruption. Retail, at both high and low ends, has flourished around the aggregation of populations; companies like Walmart or Saks erected physical stores where big groups of people lived, and the folks who frequented each location were a largely homogenous lot.

"Thirty years ago, your neighbor would have been just like you, but now you might have more in common with someone who lives in Sao Paolo or Singapore," Lenihan says. "Now you need to think about how to build a business not based on geography, but by firing all the rifle shots across the massive 2.5 billion people connected online. It's a complete reorganization of the entire world's social graph happening as a result of globalization and connectivity."

Lenihan flew to India eight years ago and was struck when the twenty-eight-year-old junior employee showing him around a company began speaking in perfect English about American pop culture. "I asked him, 'How long did you live in the States?' and he said, 'I've never been there in my life,'" Lenihan recounts. "You look at that disruption and think about how societies will be aggregated differently. They're no longer based on location, and entire industries have been based on location before. What do you do when the entire underpinning of an industry is taken out?"

These disruptions are creating opportunities for women. Lenihan teaches an undergraduate class in entrepreneurship called "Ready, Fire, Aim!" at New York University's Stern School of Business, and half his class is women. He says it's become much easier to find female role models to feature as guest speakers. More importantly, he—a white male in his late forties—predicts his best students, the ones who will create really valuable businesses, will be women. "Computers are now part of their world, so there's no sense that they don't know or shouldn't do anything," he says.

"There's this blissful ignorance about past prejudices, even more than ten years ago. You just see they can do it."

Still, venture capitalists are quick to say their investments are merit-based and gender-blind. They're businesses, not nonprofits, and they're not going to waste time on quota-fillers and charity cases. "My partners, co-investors, and LPs are almost all men," says Amanda Reed, a partner at Palomar Ventures, a venture capital firm based in California. "My investments in women entrepreneurs are not done as favors. They're done with men's support and participation. I may be using my connections, but we all make money."

With the help of their networks, female digerati have managed to differentiate themselves, and in the process, they've become legitimate horses to bet on. It's this pulsing pipeline of young women with support from their elders, plus increasing amounts of press and venture funding, that will drive this trend from a dirt road to a multilane superhighway.

"I never focus on gender; I just focus on metrics and delivering on the business. Maybe I am representative of my generation. I think women are this powerful audience. We're not second-class citizens; we're out there kicking butt," Alexa von Tobel says. "I've been so lucky, I want to give back to everyone, young and old. I want to spread the goodwill. I want to let other women know that we can take risks and recognize it can be very fruitful. The only thing that will ever hold me back is not being prepared, not doing my homework.

"I'm grateful for the women who've come before me. They've made it so I can feel this way," she continues. "But we are the new guard. We have networks that are both male and female, and we're going to help our peers. We're out there creating a meritocracy and we are going to change the world."

LADY 2.0

I n Silicon Valley, the ladies have balls and drive Porsches. They've been changing the world for a while. At least that's what Deborah Perry Piscione found when she moved west in 2006. In that nexus of innovation, it wasn't the weather or wealth that amazed her. It was the women.

Piscione was in her late thirties and had built a strong career in media and foreign relations on the East Coast. She'd labored in New York and D.C. and now, having just given birth to her third child, she sought to launch an online magazine for women. In Silicon Valley, she met one influential woman who, in a flip of dominoes, introduced her to another and another, until she found herself one night at Heidi Roizen's Atherton home. Or, more specifically, Roizen's guest house, built for entertaining on her estate. Rumor had it a secret tunnel linked the two outposts, but that night Piscione only got so far.

Roizen, the trailblazing technology entrepreneur and venture capitalist, had been asked by Tesla executives to host a focus group to make their sedan more appealing to women. She'd lassoed friends and friends of friends, who descended on her Spanish Mediterranean manse for finger food and Rombauer wine, Roizen's favorite, from her 1,500-bottle cellar.

When Piscione pulled into Roizen's gated compound, she could hardly maneuver her Mercedes between wall-to-wall sports cars. This had been billed as a girl-party, so who owned all the studly wheels?

"I had never seen so much testosterone! Heidi was the queen bee, but there were some very powerful VCs in the room, and none of these women was hesitant to speak. There was competition, but in a positive way. They were so bold," Piscione says. "Back east, my whole network was men, but here there's this big group of incredible, fearless women. They rise a lot more quickly in their careers, and they support each other. They've made their own money and they take risks. There's such a disconnect between the two coasts."

> All around her, Piscione witnessed women taking chances with their money and careers, opening not only their Rolodexes but also their wallets for one another.

Suddenly, it was like learning a new word: She saw it everywhere. Piscione is from Miami, a hotbed of splash and flash, but she had never seen so many Porsches in her life, and certainly not with women behind the wheels. Yet here, at every corner, ladies were rocking 911s. "These women are not only in the driver's seat," she says, "but have the balls to go with it."

Even weirder? The women had power—their collective wealth was in the billions—but they wore it lightly. They relaxed. They hung out. They were friends. And they were open to meeting and absorbing transplants like Piscione. It all seemed so effortless, too good to be true. Where were all the bitches?

"I was so used to people tearing me down behind my back in Washington. You don't get that out here, and it just took me a while to get used to it. If I were to go back to D.C., I think I would put my mask back on to protect myself," she says. "Maybe part of it's the weather. Maybe you're not fighting in the subway or fighting in business because you're not the only woman in the room. All of that is absent here, so maybe women don't need that body armor. We can feel free to be who we really are, to help and give and nurture. It felt like a bond of sisterhood."

All around her, Piscione witnessed women taking chances with their money and careers, opening not only their Rolodexes but also their wallets for one another. She wanted to be a part, so she snagged herself a Panamera and prepared to grow a pair. "I would have been embarrassed to drive a Porsche back east, but it's a car I've wanted my whole life. One day I woke up and said screw it," she continues. "I appreciate driving precision cars. I'm not driving 80 miles per hour, but I'm a car person and I appreciate performance and efficiency. The car is very much in sync with my personality."

Within eighteen months of her arrival, Piscione raised $5 million from a single female investor and became cofounder of a production company, Desha Productions, and its accompanying website, BettyConfidential.com. And all the while, she studied these advanced creatures, with their super-glued networks and willingness to roll the dice. What made these ladies tick, and how had they evolved?

A Culture of Risk Taking

"It's a culture of risk taking," says Sue Siegel, the CEO of healthyimagination, G.E.'s $6 billion global healthcare initiative, and a former partner at the venture capital firm Mohr Davidow Ventures, based in Menlo Park. "Entrepreneurship is so embedded here. It's what everyone talks about. If you don't participate, you're on the outside. When I did a counseling event at my son's school, every single junior in his high school class knew what a venture capitalist was."

Siegel says that when she first joined Mohr Davidow after having been an entrepreneur, she tried to determine why 40 percent of venture investing occurred in the Bay Area, rather than in Boston or other major cities. Like Silicon Valley, Boston has world-class universities and research facilities, and in Boston, founders also benefit from infrastructure and support—lawyers, accountants, HR executives, and consultants willing to work on a project basis to buttress the budding entrepreneur. If neither research resources nor professional scaffolding was the distinguishing factor, then what was so special about her home region?

Siegel decided it was a deep and ingrained ethos, a set of unique cultural norms developed after three decades of companies congealing and falling apart. Astounding victories and cringe-inducing failures are everywhere, so it's second nature for locals to gamble on start-ups. "Boston has the Brahmin bow-tie society and status thing. Failure in Boston is unacceptable. You cannot fail and feel good about it," Siegel says. "But you fail in Silicon Valley and the next VC hires you because they see you've learned from it. They see you're not going to repeat your mistakes now that you understand the landmines. Look at Google. They got turned down by so many venture firms and they're proud of it. Here we wear failure as a badge of experience and honor. I survived!"

Heidi Roizen, who's mixed with the likes of Bill Gates and Steve Jobs, agrees, saying Valley denizens have no choice but to hustle. "I was employee number one at a start-up, and if I didn't make meaningful connections, follow up, and sell things, I wasn't going to eat. When you're in an entrepreneurial situation, you have to motivate people and you have to reciprocate and be helpful to others," she says. "Life here is in constant beta, and that's a really good thing. We constantly have to reinvent ourselves because of the way the world is evolving. The world changes so rapidly now that everything you know and any skill set you have will be obsolete in a few years."

> *Organizations are not networks. Organizations are opportunities to find people to build your networks. —Kathi Lutton*

Silicon Valley is the crucible. Its singular entrepreneurial ecosystem encourages everyone—and women, disproportionately—to revel in possibilities. Because every aspect of one's career is a variable, because instability is the only constant, employees don't have the same allegiance to organizations. Networks are the stimuli for intellectual exchange and the conduits to jobs. Networks are the superstructures above organizations and the lattice below, there to catch entrepreneurs when they fall.

"Organizations are not networks. Organizations are opportunities to find people to build your networks," says Kathi Lutton, a principal at the law firm Fish & Richardson, where for four years she led the litigation group and served on the management committee. "I do not define my network by my organization. Why define your network by narrow criteria, like an organization, when you can draw the circle wider? You can define the world the way you want it to look."

Lutton, who began her career as an electrical engineer at G.E., finds that after living in Silicon Valley and participating in events such as the Fortune "Most Powerful Women" summit, her scope is much broader. "I know people who are well outside my field," she says. "It's so rare to meet a lawyer now. Each new person I meet might be somehow related to my business—VC, private equity, entrepreneurs—but I also include my hairdresser who knows book publishers. Now, when I meet somebody new, I can think of so many people who can help them."

And because this wide web is a source of new business, it increases Lutton's clout in her company. "There are mostly men in my law firm, so I'm not as powerful because of that dynamic. But when I define my network differently, it becomes much more powerful," she continues. "Someone commented recently that I have tons of business because I'm friends with people. But isn't that what guys have been doing for years?"

Clearly, a select few can unite through the Fortune "Most Powerful Women" conference, but what about the average Jane? Lutton insists connections aren't hard to build. Women just have to go out and grab them, exactly as they've been doing in Silicon Valley for decades. "It's not actually that difficult to get involved in it. People don't come to my events just for me, but because of the other people they know will be there."

Lutton recently met a man whose daughter is a sophomore in college, and she told him to put the girl in touch. "She could do so much right now to create amazing opportunities for herself. You don't already need to be tied into a network. What if she reached out and started hosting events for alumnae women who are doing really well? She could make herself the center," Lutton says. "A lot of people say 'I'm not powerful' or 'I don't have those connections,' but you have to put yourself in a place to make them."

Silicon Valley is a place where college girls can make themselves the center of the universe. There's no notion of status or society or lineage, and many of the wealthiest "locals" are fresh off the boat. While some insist it's not a completely level playing field, this region remains the biggest meritocracy the United States has to offer. In chaos lies the opportunity.

By founding or joining start-ups, women see an opportunity to be judged on the merit of their ideas rather than their gender. "The tech industry as a whole has been one of the most long-standing meritocracies. The start-up is the door to the palace. It's always been the path for innovators to fast-track themselves to success," says Amanda Reed, the venture capitalist, who sees women streaming into the Valley in record numbers. "For women, there's no climbing the corporate ladder or doing time in a male world. West Coast women don't have that 'I win–you lose' competitiveness—the blue suits, the hard shells."

Reed has been part of a dinner group of female VCs called, in jest, the No Whiners Club, and while the ladies talk about capital structures and deals, they also compare shoes and clothes. During their collective Baby Boom, they threw each other showers and laughed about the indignities of LP tours while hugely pregnant. "These aren't opposite sides of our personalities," Reed says. "They're fully integrated parts of who we are. We're not man-haters, and we're not just pro-women. We're women who are happy and fulfilled."

Reed, who is in her mid-forties, was raised in Silicon Valley, and her father was an entrepreneur in the early days of the PC revolution. She spent all but three years of her career close to home, but she says her former Dartmouth classmates who remained on the East Coast tell a different tale. "I live under an equality bubble that sits over the San Francisco Bay area. I never felt the glass ceiling growing up and working in Silicon Valley," she says. "When I went back to my college reunion, I had a lack of things to contribute when my friends wanted to commiserate about the plight of the sisterhood, because I'd never felt it."

This bolsters Deborah Perry Piscione's assertion that Silicon Valley women owe their moxie to insularity. Many were raised in the area and never left, or attended Stanford and then grew roots. "They have no idea what business or networking is like on the East Coast. They are so isolated that they are not influenced by any negative fear factors—only positive reinforcement," Piscione reflects. "A parallel is the country of Iceland. It's so isolated [that] they have a very rich and pure culture."

Despite the bombshell sex discrimination lawsuit filed in May 2012 by Ellen Pao, a junior partner at Kleiner Perkins (one of the most illustrious VC firms), Reed says Silicon Valley gals are less organized because they don't have a common enemy. They don't feel the same oppression. Instead, these ladies credit male colleagues with providing milieus where they can thrive.

"Our work/life dynamic is just different. We work with male partners who take the afternoons off to coach their sons' football teams. They'll say, 'I can talk to you after 6 PM tonight, but not before,'" says Reed, lively and blond in her pale pink jacket. "Here in the Valley, you don't feel like you have to hide the fact that you're a girl. My partners would stop marathon Monday partner meetings and check e-mails while I went to use my breast pump. As long as I'm making money for the fund, they make it an easy place for me to work."

Who are these guys, anyway? These daddies at school and on the playground? Fathers in Silicon Valley aren't shadow figures racing off at dawn and tiptoeing home late at night. They're woven into the fabric of each day. How? Just like Heidi Messer said, entrepreneurship is consuming but flexible, and founders who've hit pay dirt early in life have options. One spouse can decide to take one or two or five years off, or parents can take turns as primary breadwinners. They can afford to be around for their kids. And in a society where inventors are kings, their decrees rule. They supply archetypes the masses now emulate.

"You see much higher engagement of men with their children out here. There's a true culture of co-parenting," Piscione says. "When you've made a huge pot of money, you have the luxury of being hyperengaged. You have the luxury of time. And for women, when you have that level of support from your husband, it's easier."

Silicon Valley promotes better partnerships between the sexes, both at home and in the workplace. As a result, when women are disgruntled in their careers, they're more likely to vote with their feet. "Why stay in a job where you're unhappy? If you're good, you leave and it's their loss," Amanda Reed says. "We work seamlessly with men. We appreciate men. I've had the chance to mentor both my partners' daughters. If it weren't for the men we work with being pro-women, we wouldn't be in a position to invest in their daughters' companies. Their mothers said, 'I kicked the door open, sweetie. Now you run through it.'"

California Girls (I Wish They All Could Be . . .)

Valley Girls are old pros at kicking down doors. There, ladies are version 2.0.

"California is the fifth-largest economy in the world. You can't tell me women can't make it in a place where Meg Whitman and Carly Fiorina have paved the way," Reed says, referring to the current and past heads of Hewlett-Packard. Meg and Carly may have not linked arms and skipped toward the Emerald City, but other movers and shakers did. Even way back when.

Reed recounts a time she was working in sales and marketing at her second or third start-up and was invited as a friend's date to Heidi Roizen's company holiday party. "Heidi was out of school making tons of money when I was a teenager, and I remember walking into that room and seeing her in black leather pants that laced up the sides. I took one look and was like, 'Holy smokes!' I was instantly inspired."

Years later, when Reed was flourishing herself, she donned similar saucy trousers at an event hosted by Roizen's friend, another celebrated female VC. "I said, 'You tell Heidi these pants are for her,'" she laughs. "It took me all these years to wear black leather pants to a Christmas party and say, 'Bring it!' That moment of confidence comes from other women who are clearly acting confident. She had the confidence to be fun. Heidi is a beacon to other women. She doesn't take shit from anybody."

Still, Roizen says that when she sports the latest fashions, it's not because she's making a statement; she's just as often seen in sweats. "It's not about how expensive your shoes are. Jimmy Choos are fine, but so are flip-flops," she explains. "We're very loose here because it's about merit, not about some formality. We feel comfortable showing up who we are." When Roizen travels—as she did to a recent Berkshire Hathaway meeting in Omaha, and then to London—she often has to remind herself to step it up. "I work globally, so I had to go through my closet and say, 'A businesswoman in London doesn't wear Silicon Valley clothes.' When I go somewhere else, I have to think about protocol."

So potent is the lore around Roizen you'd think she was superhuman. This woman's a techie, but she's more than the sum of her bits. After leaving the executive committee of the National Venture Capital Association, Roizen created SkinnySongs, a workout soundtrack that landed her on CNN and the *Martha Stewart Show*. She belly dances. She once imported camels from Reno, Nevada, for a party on her estate. The entertainment home on that former property was built as a casbah with a hand-carved, hand-painted dome dispatched from Morocco.

With multidimensional role models like these, Silicon Valley executives of both sexes are less likely to differentiate between male and female behavior. Good business is good business, no matter who's executing. Roizen and her girls work hard and play hard. They know how to have fun. They strive for excellence—and if they do it with a pedicure in heels, then all the better.

"We have to find a way to be successful that doesn't compromise us as women. I'm lucky because I get to make a meaningful contribution to business, but I can also spend time with my family and my dog and my friends," Roizen says. "It's like when you speak other languages, but it's hard because you're ultimately thinking in English. When you're a woman trying to speak and act like a man, you're expending energy on that while other people are just focusing on the work. If you have to put energy into being someone you're not just to fit in, you'll always be at a disadvantage."

While Roizen remains a polestar and "fairy godmother" for so many women, she's not unique in Silicon Valley. In the late 1990s, long before women's groups formed an explicit power base, ladies were weaving webs, shutting down computers, and taking time away from frantic schedules to meet quarterly for dinner. They included Meg Whitman, who was then CEO of eBay; Joy Covey, then CFO of Amazon.com; Kim Polese, then CEO of Marimba, an Internet-based software solutions pioneer; Dana Evan, then CFO of VeriSign, a provider of Internet infrastructure services; Penny Herscher, then CEO of Simplex Solutions, an electronic design automation firm serving the semiconductor industry; and Gigi

Brisson, a founder and partner at Attractor Investment Management, which invests in technology companies. Each was one of the top female executives in her company, if not the only one.

"It was a blend of social and business interactions," explains Evan, who scoots around town in a convertible Maserati, her long blond hair trailing in a jet stream. "It was: 'What's going on in your company right now? How are you managing growth? Who are your investors? What are you doing to raise more capital?'" Jokingly christened Babes in Boyland after a boozy night at a Menlo Park restaurant, the women didn't go into dinner asking what they could get out of it. There were no precise goals or rules, but just like ladies of The Vault and 4C2B, the "Babes" saw benefits.

> "I have no time for the 'woe is us, men are so awful, it's not fair.' But if the conversation is constructive . . . you can have a lot of fun with women because you can be more relaxed."—Penny Herscher

Penny Herscher met one of her next company's early investors through the group, and Evan eventually sold one of VeriSign's payment services businesses to PayPal, which was owned by Whitman's eBay. At the time, eBay was already a customer of VeriSign and the transaction occurred later, in 2005, but Evan recalls that when VeriSign started looking at potential buyers, it was much easier to reach out to someone she knew socially as well as professionally. "That transaction didn't come out of our get-togethers, but our dinners helped facilitate the dialogue and moved the transaction along at certain points in time," Evan says. "Having personal ties in business only accelerates and enables deal making."

"It was so validating when we started organizing these dinners. It was incredibly helpful to meet with other women, telling funny stories about the absurdities of our lives, the way people interacted with us," says Herscher, who is in her early fifties and sold Simplex for $300 million in 2002. "As long as those gatherings don't become a pity party. I have no time for the 'woe is us, men are so awful, it's not fair.' But if the conversation is constructive, which it was, you can have a lot of fun with women because you can be more relaxed."

Still, Herscher, who is now president and CEO of FirstRain—a provider of search and analytics technology based in San Mateo—insists these women got to powerful positions because they're mercenary and smart with their time and resources. "They're networking with other powerful women because it's fun and it appeals to them, but also because it gives them an advantage over their male competition," she says. "This isn't philanthropy. It's capitalism at work. "

That gutsy female vanguard brought forth a cabal of "It Girls" who now dominate the Silicon Valley scene. Sheryl Sandberg, the COO of Facebook, is the leader of the pack, the rising Roizen. She's an almost-billionaire taking up women's issues as her personal mandate, presiding over a firm that gives new parents $4,000 in spending money. She's announcing that she leaves work at 5:30 PM to eat dinner with her family. She's on stage at TED events, counseling young women "don't leave before you leave," don't mentally check out of work in anticipation of having children. And though she was thrashed for playing dead as Facebook went public without a single woman or person of color on its board, perhaps she angled from the inside. Sandberg was appointed a director just a month later.

And every four to six weeks, she's at home, surrounded by plucky gal-pals. Sandberg hosts salons in her Atherton house, where audacious dames like Gloria Steinem and Geena Davis consort with Sandberg's band of Valley Girls, plus the rising female talent they're grooming. Sandberg's children scamper around the room.

Sukhinder Singh Cassidy, a regular at these salons, says her friendships with women like Sandberg and Theresia Gouw Ranzetta came about organically. The first time Cassidy met Sandberg, Sandberg was about to move to Silicon Valley and interviewed with Cassidy's firm. Ranzetta was a junior venture capitalist, and they all attended the same parties for single young techies. "We all grew up together," says Cassidy, who is now in her early forties and is married with three kids. "We were all single, young, and starting in our careers. We all got married, had babies, and hit career inflections at the same points. We all experienced life changes together. There's a group of forty women who know each other really well and have become powerful together, so there's this dynamic tribing going on. It's become the norm."

Sandberg and Cassidy also worked together at Google, where Cassidy led a women's leadership group. She, like Sandberg, consciously cultivates female protégées. Most recently, she joined the board of a former intern's company, a subscription clothing service for women, and introduced its founder to her first angel investor. "I'm a lean-forward kind of person, and I have a passion for commerce, particularly women's commerce. I enjoy building anything, and I live in a place where it's possible to have an idea and make it a reality," she says. "All of these women could be at hard-core tech companies. They're all smart enough to succeed in any hard-core industry. I like that they have the courage to marry tech and passion, to succeed in this."

For Cassidy, helping other women isn't charity since she benefits as well. "I spend time with smart, amazing people," she continues. "And do I care more about helping a woman founder? Yeah, I do."

One look at Cassidy, Sandberg, and Ranzetta makes clear they're a new breed. Sandberg has crossed the barrier into pop culture, as she's covered in both the *New York Times* and *Vogue*. As for Cassidy, when she struts into a café in Manhattan's East Village to pitch her new venture, JOYUS—which she describes over lattes and macarons as "flash sale's next step, content plus entertainment"—she's clad in a silver dress topped by a necklace of grand stars in primary colors. She shifts long black hair to one side before diving into a detailed account of culling analytics.

> *With cover girls like this, is smart the new hot?*

Meanwhile, at the height of her career, Ranzetta of Accel Partners is the last person to veil her femininity. She's known for being fashion-forward, favoring brands like Dolce & Gabbana with the current season's waist-cinching belts and over-the-knee stiletto boots. She lists "fashionista" in her Twitter profile. In October 2008, she appeared in a sexy glamour shot—white button-down open dangerously low, shiny dark hair sweeping past her shoulders, lips parted—on the cover of *Fortune*. In April 2011, Ranzetta wore a chic red frock on the front page of the *New York Times* Sunday Business section. And there she was again a few months later in *Fortune*, glancing confidently backward, her long limbs bronzed as Jennifer Aniston's, outstretched as she exited a town car.

With cover girls like this, is smart the new hot?

Ranzetta's appeal has proved good PR for her firm. This woman is uncompromising and committed, and she has the Ivy League degrees and engineering qualifications to prove it. She travels 100 days per year. But she's bringing sexy back to business on her own terms, not in some *Mad Men* parody of allure. Her looks don't undermine her intelligence; they're just one element of a sleek, branded package she is using to Accel's, and her own, advantage.

Ranzetta, Cassidy, and Sandberg are all poster children for what some have called "feminine feminism," an equal pairing of brains and beauty. They're professional, always—no showcase of knockers and knees—yet they don't have to look like men to be taken seriously. Bluestockings begone.

It's a far cry from the early 1990s, when Ranzetta was sent home from her entry-level job at Bain & Company for wearing a pantsuit. At the time she was an analyst fresh out of Brown University and had dressed practically for that day's winter storm. She had no client meetings and would be behind her desk all day, but still her superiors told her to change. Better to brave a blizzard in nylons and a skirt.

Now she makes her own choices and presents a new paradigm for women coming up. "Sometimes I'm still the only woman in the room, so who are they going to compare me to? Should I wear the khaki-pants-blue-button-down uniform?" she laughs. "I wear what I want. Some days I wear jeans, and some days I wear dresses. I like dresses."

"Alley to the Valley"

After Deborah Perry Piscione launched her company, she joined 85 Broads and started talking to Janet Hanson, who'd founded the women's network on the East Coast. Silicon Valley, they agreed, felt like an alternate universe. Who were these intellectual powerhouses who actually looked like girls? How was it their husbands donned baby slings while they sped around in high-performance vehicles?

Piscione and Hanson felt like anthropologists discovering a foreign species, and they wanted to share their findings. They hoped to bring their Atlantic sisters to bathe in these Pacific waters, if only for a day. So, on the evening of November 10, 2010, a valet eased Piscione's Porsche Panamera up to the entrance of the Rosewood Sand Hill Hotel in Menlo Park, the heart of Silicon Valley.

"This car is a work of art," Hanson said, hitching a ride to dinner. "It could eat us for lunch."

The two women were meeting in person for the first time after months on the phone planning a "pretty hefty schmoozefest." They'd organized the first "Alley to the Valley" conference to introduce twenty-five self-made women from the East Coast, many with net worths north of $100 million, to their West Coast counterparts. The event was invitation-only and each woman had paid $1,500, not including hotel and airfare, for the opportunity to expand her network and bridge the coastal divide.

East Coasters also aimed to start thinking and investing more entrepreneurially. "There are all of these women who made tons of money and now are not doing anything with it," Piscione says. East Coast women may have attended top business schools and reached the apex of corporate America, but "they're not making their mark." They are losing relevance, Piscione says, in the "new economy."

For the most part, wealthy Eastern women inherited their money, got it through divorce, or toiled for thirty years to fill the coffers. Many spent decades fighting for parity as the only woman in a particular department on Wall Street, and many feel like they've bled for every last cent. They're corporate gals, not entrepreneurs, and they lack the networks and knowledge base to invest in new ventures. Tech just hasn't been part of the Eastern vernacular.

As a result, East Coast gals are tighter with their cash and, while they may be highly philanthropic, their money is managed by outsiders. "It takes longer to make it in finance," Hanson says. "Compensation is still reasonably obscene here, but it's not a windfall, like if you were employee number five or even 500 at Google. In that case, you're willing to back other start-ups because you see the enormous potential."

From Hanson's vantage point in Greenwich, Connecticut, the East Coast is hemorrhaging while Valley Girls chant "Dolla Dolla Bill Y'all" between wheatgrass shots on their mountain bikes. It's just one more example of how California and New York have never been in sync. When the first tech bubble burst, New Yorkers were nearly immune. And while Californians felt the aftershocks of 9/11, they didn't taste the ashes and smell it in the streets. Now the West Coast is taking the latest financial crisis in stride.

"The West Coast is brand new in so many ways, and everyone seems to be having an awfully good time. It reminds me of Wall Street culture back in the '80s where the great firms were privately held and the passion for building and innovating was unbelievable," Hanson says. "The amount of real emotional and financial pain on the East Coast is off the charts. It's been brutal to be part of the sad story, living it here. Instead of just giving up, I want to stay ahead of the curve. Rather than licking our wounds and wondering how much our 401(k)s are down today, we need to do something new. We need to partner with the West Coast. It's a cultural, entrepreneurial revolution. It's the gold rush, and we want in."

Wanting in is one thing, but fitting in is another.

In preparation for "Alley to the Valley," one woman wonders about the attire. Will it be like a wedding destined for doom, where ushers know just by looking which guests are on the bride's side or the groom's? Or like the failed Time Warner–AOL merger, which in 2000 was the largest deal in history and now stands as a cautionary tale? Some say its downfall was presaged when the chiefs of each shop arrived at their press conference, comically in the garb of the other: Steve Case in a dapper suit, Jerry Levin ready for Casual Friday, neither one looking comfortable or quite right.

> *Around a U-shaped table in a hotel ballroom, they'll let their hair down. Literally. Someone will say she's never seen so much long, flowing hair at a business function.*

But at the "Alley to the Valley" kickoff dinner in 2010 at the home of Linda Law, a Silicon Valley real estate mogul, the delegations are uniformly clad in cocktail dresses and elegant separates. "I love your dress," someone says, fingering the wool of a new friend's sheath. "Is that this season or last?" The women mingle and marvel at Law's art collection, and the following day, around a U-shaped table in a hotel ballroom, they'll let their hair down. Literally. Someone will say she's never seen so much long, flowing hair at a business function. There will be serious debate, yes, but it will feel like the female equivalent of loosening one's tie. No one seems out for blood.

And really, what's a women's event without priapic indulgence? Since they're not going to strip clubs, at least the girls can talk sex toys. At one lunch table, someone will be funding Jimmyjane, a purveyor of high-end vibrators and "pleasure sets," and the ladies will laugh, going back and forth about models they prefer, which are too loud, which are least likely to get caught in travel. They'll lean in to share the "friends and family" discount code: "Independence."

There will be cards exchanged and moments of community.

Yet at that inaugural dinner, discrepancies are clear, and it doesn't take long for factions to emerge. Like when Barbara Byrne, in her late fifties and one of the most senior women on Wall Street, tells a story about her daughter, who was an intern and the only female at a start-up in New York when she called her mom to say that all the employees were going to an investor dinner. She'd been excluded but told to make the reservation. Byrne is livid.

"I said, 'Fuck them! Son of a bitch!'" she bellows, stabbing her finger in the air. "I told her to show up and when the investor sees she's the only woman in the room, he'll want to sit next to her. This is my kid. I want to shoot them!"

Kohl-rimmed eyes are bulging, eyebrows raised in parabolas of shock. Byrne knows she has the ball, and she's running down the field. She persists, recounting a time when a colleague called her a castrating bitch on the trading floor. "I came out with a pair of shears." She extends long arms over her head, relishing the recap. "And I screamed 'Grrrruuuuuber!!'" Byrne bares her teeth, savoring the offending man's name. "You gotta go to war!"

When her tirade ends, it's like a balloon deflating. Women shrug and shift their gaze. "But when you go to war, the way it's perceived if you're a woman. . . ." says a venture capitalist and former entrepreneur, shaking her head. Someone excuses herself to find the bathroom.

It's dinnertime, clearly not the moment for a battle with Byrne, who raised four kids while rising to be a vice chair at Lehman, and now at Barclays. But it's not like the West Coast gals have been neutered and declawed. There are countless ways to be a successful woman, and not all of them require guerilla tactics.

Byrne later laments that fewer women are coming to the Street, but on nights like this, who can blame them for snubbing the sword and breastplate and trying to rock the casbah instead?

THE COMFORT
FORMULA

Here's the rub: Nobody likes a loser. No one, regardless of gender, wants to be lumped in with a second-rate crowd when she's working so hard to succeed. And no one wants to be passed over for promotions or stretch assignments because she's perceived as a whiner. Historically, the most talented women shunned clusters with a scent of self-pity or a whiff of wallowing. In the early days, as Joan Lau of Azelon Pharmaceuticals said, businesswomen tried to conform and fit in with men. They sported short hair, "dorky ties," and power suits. Many wouldn't consider joining all-female groups, which were deemed down-market, but instead joined trade groups to be with guys who could help them get ahead.

"For many years, I would never go to a girls' meeting. I have to go where the action is, where the power is," says Heidi Roizen, who in September 2012 joined the board of Daily Mail and General Trust, a British media conglomerate, as the first female director in the company's 116-year history. "I have definitely been to some meetings in the past where I felt like it was a bunch of women in the room complaining about why they didn't have it as good as men. That's a nonstarter for me."

On the heels of *L'affaire* Pao at Kleiner Perkins, Anne-Marie Slaughter's *Atlantic* dirge ("Why Women Still Can't Have It All"), and the backbiting over Marissa Mayer's capacity to swagger as Yahoo CEO while swaddling her newborn, there's an air of dyspepsia. Gender fatigue prevails. While some gals celebrate the creation of their own "golf game," most denounce the "women's ghetto." They say supportive male bosses and mentors have been instrumental in their rise. Working in isolation is no option when men still hold the keys to power—97 percent of Fortune 500 CEO positions and 85 percent of corporate board seats, to be exact. And the suggestion that gender should inform investments insults women's business acumen, as if implying they use pink dollars instead of green.

"I am so much more interested in the science of the companies I take public—if they're changing an industry and taking the ball forward—than I am in whether their boards and management teams are male, female, black, white, green, from Mars," says Cristina Morgan, a technology banker and vice chair at JPMorgan Chase. "It's like telling me someone has red hair. Big deal. I think the fact that I was born in Florence, Italy, is more interesting than the fact that I'm female."

Morgan maintains that building relationships with both men and women is something successful businesspeople do as a matter of course. And because she's been a banker for more than thirty years and taken more than 250 companies public, Morgan knows a ton of folks. She regularly recommends people for jobs and boards, provided they're qualified. "Success begets success, and if some of these connections are a total bust and don't make people money, then they will not continue," she says. "It's about chemistry, not particularly if they're male or female."

But when you look at her stats, it's clear Morgan has proposed a lot of ladies for a lot of different jobs. Morgan doesn't go out of her way to champion women, but perhaps because she is a leader who *happens* to be female, she's more likely to see other women as potential leaders too. Perhaps women come more easily to mind because they're friends, or because Morgan runs into them at events like the Fortune "Most Powerful Women" summit.

"This happens to me all the time," she admits. "Twenty years to learn, twenty years to earn, twenty years to return: That's your career. I'm a natural magnet for professional women because of my business, profession, and age. I have so many women friends with backgrounds and résumés and capability to do all of this that a lot of people ask me. I went to an all-girls Catholic high school, so naturally if your friends are women—you laugh at the same jokes, you have a lot in common—those are the people you'll think of. I can name dozens of women I know, like, and interact with, and of course I would recommend them if I thought the chemistry was right."

It's like matchmaking, she says, and when making both business and personal connections, you're looking for the right fit. Character and personality obviously come into play. "Just because someone is pretty and skinny and likes skiing doesn't mean she'll be right for your friend. I apply all of those same judgments to my women friends as I do to my men friends," Morgan expands. "A lot of women I'm nice to, but I wouldn't recommend to put gas in my car. When you recommend someone for a job or a board, you're really speaking for that person. All of these people are in my world. I'm just trafficking in logic patterns, recommending professionals for professional reasons. And a lot of times they happen to be girls."

Bitters Belong in the Drinks

One of Morgan's girls is Dana Evan, a member of the Babes in Boyland who was the founding CFO of VeriSign when Morgan, among others, proposed her as a board member and audit committee chair for both MySQL, an open source database company, and Omniture, a Web analytics business. Evan joined both boards in 2006, and she now sits on six corporate boards, two of which are public—which is a rarity for anyone, male or female.

Another gal is Karen White, whom Morgan met when White was a senior executive at Oracle in the 1990s. They stayed in contact when White moved to Pequot, a private equity firm, and in 2007, Morgan suggested White as a potential board member for SolarWinds, a network management software company in Austin, Texas. Instead of joining the board, White ended up joining the company as head of worldwide corporate and business development. SolarWinds went public in 2009, and today the company has an equity market capitalization of $3.9 billion.

Both White and Morgan say the recommendation had nothing to do with gender and everything to do with White's talent and expertise. They had known each other for fifteen years and worked successfully side-by-side by the time the SolarWinds position came up. Not to mention that SolarWinds wasn't looking for a woman; the company wanted a seasoned executive, and White checked all the boxes.

She had a history of success. In 1993, White was the thirty-year-old CEO of Egis, an international firm focused on networking and communications technology, when she met Larry Ellison, the chairman and CEO of Oracle, on a plane from D.C. to California. He happened to be her seatmate, and they spent hours talking technology trends, speculating about the ways networks would evolve and how Oracle might exploit the opportunities. "I want you to come work for me," Ellison said as they disembarked. He pursued White for four months until she agreed, and only after Ellison understood her priorities.

White was a single mom, and she was willing to relocate and travel internationally, but her daughter would come along. "It wasn't a condition. It was just a statement of fact," she says. "I said, 'I've got a kid and she comes with. I'll make it all work, but I want that to be clear.' And he said, 'There's no issue,' and it never was." In fact, when trying to recruit White from the East Coast, Ellison drove her past the elementary school his children attended—where a library was named after him, and where her daughter would go if White accepted the position. "You can opt in or opt out," she continues, "and if you say explicitly how it's going to look, they will know your bar coming in."

White worked at Oracle for seven years, departing in 2000 as senior vice president leading worldwide business development to join Pequot as a managing director, and later run technology firms. All the while, her daughter, Christina, accompanied her around the globe. White never brought along a nanny, but rather found company employees to escort Christina around each city to teach her about the local culture—an experience Christina wrote about in an essay that landed her at Yale.

Mother and daughter still talk daily and their conversations increasingly veer toward work, as Christina dove first into banking and now venture capital. One recent afternoon, over lunch at the Monkey Bar in midtown Manhattan, Christina described an office conflict and her mom leaned in and listened. Karen waited to be asked for her advice before offering, and when Christina did inquire, Karen was measured in her tone, making it clear she had faith in her daughter's abilities. Observing the interaction, it wasn't so much the love that struck a bystander as unusual, or even the evident pride. It was the tremendous mutual respect.

> *"When nine of ten executives in positions to make decisions are still male, why would you segregate yourself or favor a woman just because of gender?"—Karen White*

Still, White is pro-woman in her philanthropic work, not her professional work. "When nine of ten executives in positions to make decisions are still male, why would you segregate yourself or favor a woman just because of gender?" asks White, who became CEO of Syncplicity, a company that uses cloud computing for file management, in 2011. "Women are searching for the holy grail. There isn't one. The women I know who are really successful just think in terms of businesses, not gender, and they get folded in. There is no effective affirmative action at the senior executive level. I don't think about having an impact in business as a woman. I think about having an impact period, putting your head down and getting it done."

But talk about "feminine feminism," and talk about a product of Silicon Valley. Karen White looks like a cross between Julia Roberts and Hilary Swank, and she's kept in Olympic shape by the trainer she shares with her close friend Eric Schmidt, the former CEO and current executive chairman of Google.

On leap year 2012, White planned a last-minute dinner at the Village Pub, a neighborhood hangout in Woodside, California, whose very name is symbolic of the Valley lifestyle. It's a wood-paneled den where anything goes, where women pair ice-cube–size diamonds with Tevas and jeans, where black-hoodied oligarchs conspire in shadow, savoring $1,000 bottles of Château Lafite Rothschild with their sweetbreads vol-au-vent. This place is a "village pub" the way Mark Zuckerberg is a small business owner.

White arrived and greeted everyone—maître d', bartenders, wait staff, fellow patrons—warmly by name, before sliding comfortably into a back booth. She recommended the salad of heirloom beets with goat cheese mousse, followed by a hearty rare steak. And, for the lady famous for hosting "wine tasting sleepovers," a Gevrey-Chambertin.

She looked youthful with a bare face, wearing flip-flops adorned with little gold skulls, having come straight from a pedicure. White was preparing to attend the reading of a new play by her friend, the writer Dustin Lance Black, who won an Oscar for his screenplay for the film *Milk*. Rob Reiner was producing the event as a fundraiser for the American Foundation for Equal Rights, with an all-star cast that included Brad Pitt, George Clooney, Kevin Bacon, Martin Sheen, and Jamie Lee Curtis. White wanted to look her best.

Get her going on fashion and White's all X chromosomes. But when it comes to work, she thinks women need to stop trying to start another game, or scrum on a different field. And when she ascended the stage before thousands at the annual "EMC World Conference" in Las Vegas in May 2012, to announce the sale of Syncplicity to EMC, a $50 billion technology firm, she was clearly suited up and quarterbacking. She'd spent months of all-nighters pushing this deal through, and that evening she celebrated with her engineers, doing vodka shots and dancing to Maroon 5.

The day after the event, she sent a sweet e-mail to close friends—both male and female—announcing her good news and apologizing for being unresponsive of late. "Please forgive me for the lack of phone calls and visits, the sometimes unreturned calls and e-mails, the cancelled dinners, trips, yoga classes, runs and other plans that went sideways over the past few months. . . . I've missed you!"

Ten years ago, there were almost no women in White's professional network, even in Silicon Valley, but that needle is starting to move. Now that more than half of college graduates are women, the Old Boys' Club is naturally dissolving. "The Old Boys made sense when 85 to 95 percent of college grads were men. It's who you know. But that's different now," White expands. "As I've watched my daughter come into the workforce, she seems to have this innate ability. For her it's second nature. She's confident around executives at all levels, asking for time. When she was changing jobs, she realized she had connections with two executives in a twenty-person firm she was interested in, so she called beforehand. I didn't tell her to think that way. That's how men have always operated."

Networks are meant to extend one's scope, not restrict it. They're about integration, not isolation, after all. So White is attracted to people who share her values and sensibilities, people she trusts, be they men or women. Her networks aren't filled with people she's met at cocktail parties, or the faceless many whose business cards she's filed away. Her allegiances are stronger than that. White's network includes people she's willing to go to bat for, and who prop her up in return.

Savvy gals may unite on occasion, but they don't cut themselves off from the dudes. You won't hear these ladies fulminating, and the notion of subverting patriarchy makes them squirm. They've found allies of both sexes, and now they sponsor rising stars, regardless of gender.

Life's too short to grumble. Why be a sourpuss when there's a Pisco Sour waiting at the Village Pub? For White and her crew, bitters belong in the drinks.

Shit Happens (Even When You're Rich and Beautiful)

Within a month of that Village Pub dinner, Karen White was bowled over when a snapshot of her and George Clooney arm-in-arm headlined the itinerary for her birthday weekend. Christina had planned a surprise fiftieth birthday party in Sonoma Valley, and she'd rallied White's best girlfriends, the women she wanted there.

These are women who know that, despite the sexy accoutrements and fabulous parties, it had been a grueling year for White. They know she was still in physical therapy, that her back ached every day from a catastrophic car accident she was lucky to have survived. And they know how she traveled back and forth to D.C., sleeping at the hospice beside her cancer-stricken father—from whom she and her brother had been estranged (at her father's insistence) for most of her life, the father who had refused to meet Christina when she was born. And White's friends know she was the only one there, feeding her father ice chips and stroking his arms and holding him when he died. And they know that while all this was happening, she was called upon to steer Syncplicity as CEO when its young founders needed help.

"Karen's birthday was a very down-home thing with just a few people. She kept saying, 'I don't want a party,' but we knew it was *that kind* of party she didn't want," entrepreneur and venture capitalist Heidi Roizen says. "She wanted us, just being together."

At the time, Roizen saw what was happening to White. She knew her friend had initially been an adviser and then executive chairman of Syncplicity, and she believed that when White took the reins as CEO, she was trying to serve too many masters. Despite White's having supportive investors and capable founders, her situation was complex. She was synthesizing the aspirations of her organization's founders, the desires of the investors, her own convictions, and the market realities into a cohesive strategy. The answer wasn't yet clear. "One night after much wine was consumed, I said, 'Karen, the thing you're forgetting is that you have a tremendous amount of power. *You're* the CEO,'" Roizen recounts. "We don't go home and whine. We tell each other to get back out there and do it, kick each other in the pants. Karen wasn't telling me trade secrets of her company; she was sharing her struggles as a CEO and manager because she knew I've been there and would understand her. Unless you've been there yourself, it's hard to see a person with both great love and total objectivity."

Roizen could also relate when White's father was dying. "Karen shared a lot of personal stuff with me and it was cathartic for her because I understand her on the business side too, because I saw all the pieces," Roizen says. "At the end of the day, we're all human. Maybe we drive fancier cars. We have money and, believe me, I understand what a gift that is in this era of families living longer, kids having trouble getting jobs. I am so grateful for the income to buffer those issues. But sometimes when you have the outward trappings and feel a little intimidating, people think you shouldn't have problems. We all go through illness and challenges and loss. One time we all got together and had this incredible conversation because we were by far the biggest breadwinners in our families. What happens to your marriage when you out-earn your husband? Yeah, these are first-world problems, but they're still real."

Here Roizen speaks from experience, because when her marriage fell apart, she felt blessed to have her "Fave 5," the women who stuck by her too. "I found out about my divorce in an unusual way," she begins. Roizen was at a difficult company board meeting on the East Coast when she saw she had a voice mail from her friend Scott McNealy, the cofounder of Sun Microsystems and, at the time, its CEO. "He said, 'Call me back ASAP,'" Roizen recalls. "He's a friend, but he doesn't call me all the time, so I figured it was important."

At the next break, Roizen went to the ladies room and immediately rang McNealy. "How are you?" he asked. "I wanted to check on you to see if you're okay."

"What do you mean?" she said. "I'm fine."

"He said, 'I heard about you and David splitting up,' and I said, 'What? No we haven't.' And he said, 'Yes you have. He's left you for another woman. She's blond.' And he proceeded to tell me a bunch of information," Roizen remembers now. "My husband of twenty years had a serious relationship with someone else. He'd gone so far as to introduce her to other people and to tell others he was leaving me, but he hadn't told me. I was dumbstruck."

It was 10 AM and Roizen had to pull herself together and walk back into the board meeting. She wasn't able to get in touch with her husband for another twelve hours, but she texted and e-mailed him in the meantime, saying, "Hey, I hear you're leaving me for another woman."

> *"Other people can look at our lives and say, 'You're so lucky' because on the balance, we are. But our bad stuff hurts too. When your husband leaves you it hurts—a lot—even if you live in a mansion."—Heidi Roizen*

"At 10 that night he said, 'I'm sorry you found out that way, but our marriage is in serious trouble and I'm thinking of leaving it.' What was my immediate reaction? Call my girlfriends."

Roizen rang Ann Winblad, her friend and mentor who had been one of the first female VCs, and she called Karen White. "Ann and

Karen were there for me. I called them all the time. One of the things that makes the bond between me, Karen, and Ann so special and strong is being 'of a kind,' that we have the same work ethic, passions, and values. It's having those other women who understand you can get a phone call like that on a break in a board meeting and still have to go back in and focus for three hours. When someone can empathize with you and know exactly how shitty it feels," Roizen says. "Other people can look at our lives and say, 'You're so lucky' because on the balance, we are. But our bad stuff hurts too. When your husband leaves you it hurts—a lot—even if you live in a mansion.

"You don't necessarily go into these relationships saying, 'I'd better have someone there for me when the shit hits the fan,'" she continues. "But you want to have those people who will love you even when your biggest deal blows up and when you've lost all your money. You want the person you'd call to come get you if you were standing naked in downtown San Francisco at 3 AM. You want people who will love you even when your husband doesn't.'"

Share Your Pantyhose

Gender alone won't qualify any woman for membership in the club. For Stiletto Networks to be relevant and desirable, they must be rooted in shared experience and true sympathy—which means they must have some form of exclusivity. For Roizen, that means women who understand the "Tootsie Pop Syndrome," that she can look hard on the outside, but still be sweet and gooey on the inside.

"Karen and I have the same shoe size, so we share shoes and jewelry all the time. Ann and I were just in London shopping and she said, 'No, that doesn't look good on you.' Some girls go shopping and say, 'Oh, that looks so good.' But [Karen and Ann] are the kind of friends who tell me I look like shit and I'm grateful," Roizen says. "We're so close not because of the work we've done together, but because of what we've been through in our personal lives."

Unfortunately, countless women's groups do turn into mentoring programs. One finance executive bemoans that the once-exclusive association "100 Women in Hedge Funds has become more like 10,000 Women in Hedge Funds," with too many junior gals seeking jobs and career advice from too few women at the top. To be valuable for executive women, coteries must be peer-to-peer or invitation-only, like The Vault or 4C2B or ChIPs or PE WIN.

"It's not that senior women don't want to mentor junior women, but the purpose of this network is very different. It's about creating peer-to-peer connections, someone to reach out to if you're trying to raise a fund, if you have a deal you're working on, if you need career advice. It's someone you trust who will respond to you, who will not broadcast something that's very sensitive," Kelly Williams says of PE WIN. "Among senior women there's a craving for peer-to-peer discussion: 'How do you deal with this? What were the culture-dynamic issues when you tried to open an office in another city?' One of the biggest gaps in support is for senior women."

Many executive women, particularly in industries like finance, agree. "People assume once you become an MD [managing director], you're done. But at that point it's very difficult to share when you're having a problem. You don't want to show there's a chink in your armor," says one managing director at a global investment bank. "A lot of women have issues when they are promoted within a firm led primarily by men. When you become a partner, you expect equality. You don't expect to be left out of conversations, but you are. It's a new phenomenon, so there's not enough experience on both sides of the aisle."

Clearly, not everything has changed. Women still need a forum to discuss the intractable issues their forebears confronted decades ago. Like male colleagues who shine in paternalistic roles, but struggle with how to be equals at work. Or guys who bristle at a female boss. Or clients who assume a woman's male subordinates are in charge. Even today, this happens all the time.

Until there's true equality at senior levels, most women still tread lightly—or at least dial down the disparities. "I'm on a public company board, and everyone else on both the management team and the board is a white man," says Penny Herscher, another Babe in Boyland. "I was just the only woman in the room for two days, and you bet I sat in front of my closet and thought about what was going to be appropriate for that group. I wore all black yesterday and the day before."

For Herscher, who is in her early fifties, it's a matter of effectiveness, being attuned and knowing how to insinuate herself. "If I have been invited into the all-male sanctum and I'm carving new ground, then I try to dress and behave in a way that makes it easier to accept me. I want them to have the experience of my mind so they're comfortable bringing other women into the room," she continues. "I'm very conscious that I'm an ambassador for the next generation of women. If I'm breaking into an older white male environment, I need to match my behavior, conversation, and clothing to theirs. If I'm dressed in neon colors and talking about my shoes, I'll create an impression that women aren't as serious."

Yet here's where notions of power and exclusivity get highly nuanced. Women might publicly lament being the solitary skirt, and undoubtedly there are drawbacks. But privately, they also admit to enjoying its perks. It carries prestige, heightens the sense of individuality and distinction, and makes a lady sought after. If you're the only one showing some leg, men tend to remember you.

And many women—particularly those who've benefited from supportive Stiletto Networks—actually sympathize, off the record, with guys who want to be left alone to drink beer and play golf. They know from personal experience that when women are on their own, everything loosens up. They're at ease, with an alternate dress code and sense of decorum, as witnessed when Herscher wears a cherry-red suit and matching dangly earrings to the "Alley to the Valley" conference. Of course, it's the same for guys.

One executive woman remembers a time when a male consultant was invited to speak to her prominent girls' group and his presence completely changed the atmosphere. It just wasn't as much fun, and while the women knew this was a Catch-22, they also wished he'd never been included. "That's what men have been saying in their private clubs, in places like Augusta," she says (referring to the Augusta National Golf Club in Georgia, which did not admit its first women members until 2012). "I know why they're hanging on. I get it, and I can see both sides of that situation more clearly after feeling what it was like when a man joined our group. I don't know how not to be a hypocrite here, because it has historically excluded women from opportunity. But I understand why guys and girls want their own clubs."

Her hope is that as more women rise to positions of power, these debates become less pertinent. It's happening, she says, but we're not at the finish line. And until then, it's absurd to rejoice being separate but still unequal.

Silvia Fernandez, a senior managing director at First Republic Bank, also grappled with these issues a decade ago when she led the Internet group at Silicon Valley Bank. Her male colleagues historically hosted offsites at their CEO's beach house in Oahu, but as more women entered the field, the guys knew something had to give. How could they let the good times roll without being accused of discrimination?

In Hawaii, five or six men bunked in one huge room and used the same bathrooms. Shared accommodations were key to camaraderie. It felt like going back to college, with time condensed and experiences amplified, and men formed real friendships in a surprisingly short period of time. But guys couldn't walk around in their underwear with a bunch of chicks present, and they knew their wives would blanch at a coed spree. It just wouldn't work.

The bank's CEO offered his house to Fernandez and encouraged her to host a girls' trip of her own. The first year, Fernandez and a colleague brought three women to Oahu, and when they returned they told all their friends. Soon, others were clamoring to join them, and after a few years the women began venturing to Cabo San Lucas, Mexico, where they now rent multiple homes in a cozy subdivision. Sometimes the houses don't have enough beds, so women use blow-up mattresses and crash in a crowd. "Guys will not sleep together. Maybe they're afraid they'll become gay," Fernandez laughs. "But I've shared beds with my colleagues, and most women will share a bedroom. It's part of the camaraderie. It's like a very nice camp."

Fernandez says she originally spurned the idea of women networking alone, but then she realized something very special was happening on her excursions. "There was no golf, no cigars, not necessarily copious amounts of alcohol, but there were always massages or trips to the spa, and so much talk," she says. "It was both personal and business, and we got to know each other at a very deep level."

Each year, Fernandez organizes a game night with some diversion meant to reveal things about every woman there. Fernandez and her staff Google the women, combing page after page in search of little-known facts, or reach out to participants' assistants to determine who was a star soccer player or ballerina in high school. Fernandez then writes quizzes to match the woman to the fact or uses decks of cards with probing questions like, "If you had one day to live, what would you do?" or "What's the most bizarre investment you didn't do, but wish you had?"

The point is to get ladies talking, and after a few glasses of wine, Fernandez can barely shut them up. Without fail, they end up telling stories and admitting things like, "Yeah, I dated Bill Gates," or better yet, "Let me tell you about my double date with Bill Gates and Steve Jobs." That one brought the house down.

"You have to be really trusting in that environment because you're sharing a lot of stuff, and I became a believer in these connections. I've had women tell me they've developed really close relationships as a result of these events," Fernandez says. "I think it's because women are able to let down their guard, and it probably happens on the men's trips too. We might not necessarily like all the stuff the guys talk about, but it's the fact that they can let their hair down."

When Fernandez started planning her trips in the 1990s, none of the women had children, and now almost all of them have two. "Most of these women were the first woman partner to have a child, so in most cases the firm didn't have a maternity policy. They talked about how the partnerships were dealing with that, and in almost every case they stayed with their firms," Fernandez says. "I see with my daughter that girls just tend to share more, so it's that ability to relate on all levels, where everyone relates to the same challenges. We had four people breast-feeding one year, coming with their pumps and bringing their milk back. Where else can you find that? You're not trying to be a guy."

Fernandez spent enough time trying to be a guy to recognize the importance of female bonds. Now, when she speaks to women's groups, she tells the story of her close friend Mary Mewha, with whom she worked in the mid-1980s when they were both twenty-seven-year-old vice presidents in an otherwise male corporate banking group at First Interstate Bank. "We were so clueless," Fernandez recalls. "We were promoted before we should have been, and we'd routinely go to each other to ask the stupid questions, saying, 'Oh my God, I know I should know this, but I don't. Do you?'"

One afternoon, Fernandez was scheduled to accompany the bank's CEO to visit clients, but she had a massive run in her stocking. At the very least it would have been a distraction, and at worst perceived as unprofessional. So she yanked her friend into a restroom, where Mewha stripped down for the swap. Fernandez was good to go, and Mewha slinked around the office unkempt.

"I tell women, 'You always need to have the woman you can share your pantyhose with, someone who will literally take off her pantyhose for you,'" Fernandez says. "Of course it's not about pantyhose, which no one wears now anyway. It's about showing your insecurities, being able to ask the stupid questions, baring your soul to someone. There are few people you can do that with, and the experience has stayed with me to this day." Mewha is now a managing director at Wells Fargo's family wealth practice, and the two women remain close. Fernandez says they recently had lunch and they laughed until they cried, remembering that day.

This, Fernandez has discovered, is also the true purpose of her outings. "I think they help each one of us find the women we can share pantyhose with," she says. "We can call each other for business, or for anything else."

Otherhood, Not Motherhood

For occasional bonding trips, segregation might make sense. But on a day-to-day basis, men and women need to mix and, as Karen White says, prepare to play on coed teams. It's happening, as more boys are raised by mothers who work (yet are still involved and loving), as men strive to create opportunities for their daughters, as husbands slowly increase their share of duties at home, and as boys and girls collaborate in school. Men and women are starting, just now, to meet in the middle.

"In the '80s, people thought women were not rising to the top because they wanted to be mothers. The joke was that a lot of women denied senior slots were *not* mothers," says Edie Weiner, the futurist. "It was never about motherhood, and it never will be. It's about 'otherhood.' It's why you don't see minorities or physically challenged people at the top either. At a certain point, competence is proven and it becomes a matter of comfort. There's a need to change the comfort formula, to show that women and men are highly complementary."

Kathi Lutton at Fish & Richardson found herself testing the "comfort formula" a few years ago, when her firm began hosting a conference for female lawyers. "After I spoke on a panel, people came up and said I was so different talking in a room full of women, that I was more lively and relaxed. And I just thought, 'That's right and this feels good,'" she recounts. "It really struck me throughout my engineering career and even in law, I'd been conforming. My counterparts at other firms don't look like me. But I realized I was in a point in my career where I could be myself, so I started getting out to meet other women outside of my profession."

Even then she encountered roadblocks. Lutton says that before she presented at the Fortune "Most Powerful Women" summit, she attended a one-day training session to become a more dynamic speaker. One of the first things her coach instructed was to put up her hair. "She said, 'You need to change your look because you're too collegey,'" says Lutton, whose straight brown locks trail down her back. "The first piece of advice I got was that I looked too much like a woman. To make me seem more powerful, I needed to look like a man."

Lutton bridled and went her own way. At Fish & Richardson's principal retreat, she began to spearhead an afternoon of shoe shopping. While the male partners play basketball, the ladies hit Neiman Marcus. Then they wear their spoils to dinner that night. "We showed up in red soles. I had jeweled Manolos one year, Gucci boots another year. And the year after I started this, I was elected to the partnership of our management committee," she says. "The guys love it now. They understand and respect it."

While senior women would never counsel juvenile minions to rock the boat like this, once the older set has achieved a level of success—once they've earned that sine qua non of trust and respect—then they can begin to set a new tone. And when companies finally have enough women at high levels, female bosses can broach taboo topics and deliver thorny feedback to younger gals, too.

Such as: *You seem unfocused, like you're pulling back. Let's talk honestly about what you'll do after you get married and have kids. How might you make it work?*

Or: *That skirt is too short. That top is too tight. You can be stylish and still professional.*

You can't project gravitas while snapping gum and twirling hair.

Don't giggle like a schoolgirl.

Stop saying "like." Proper grammar and punctuation count.

Easy on the exclamation points.

Enough with the emoticons.

There's a limit on appropriate sharing: TMI, TMI, TMI.

One executive remembers some advice her brothers offered before she entered Harvard Business School. "They said, 'Don't talk like most women. Get to the point, build on the other person's point, and wrap it up,'" she laughs. "At HBS, I followed their advice and the guys would come up to me after class and say, 'It's brilliant the way you shared that.' When other women would put their hands up and talk, they made sense to me and I heard their points. But the guys were like, '*Oh my God.*'"

That kind of guidance feels like insider intel when delivered by a family member or another woman. So when a knockout like Karen White approaches a roving intern at "Alley to the Valley" to tell her, quietly and discreetly, that she should rethink her outfit—that skintight minidresses don't fly in the workplace, even in Girl World—that young lady listens. It's not her grandma talking.

Millennial girls may roll their eyes. They might grouse that their bosses or investors sound too much like their mothers, but they won't think it's an overture for sex and they won't file harassment lawsuits. That alone should be a relief to any male manager who's ever had the same thoughts, but kept his mouth shut and then not promoted an otherwise gifted young woman.

Men still can't dispense this brand of "constructive criticism" without beckoning the Lernaean Hydra of HR. When guys sling shit at male upstarts, people laugh it off, but when female subordinates need a talking-to, male bosses brace for a legal smackdown or, God forbid, the box of tissues. These chats are tricky, but when everyone avoids them, nobody wins.

Yet what about those primal urges? All this embracing femininity and looking like a girl . . . doesn't it complicate matters? Don't strappy stilettos beg for "footsie," and won't lengthy tendrils be wrenched to the nearest cave? No shock here, but the hotter the chick, the more awkward men feel.

> *Diversity is grand and liberation is divine, but "Let's Get It On" still trumps "Free to Be You and Me" at most big firms.*

Sue Siegel, the former entrepreneur and venture capitalist who is in her fifties, says that because much of her firm's work was done one-on-one at meals, she was often asked to chaperone meetings involving an older man and younger woman—just to forestall gossip. "If you end up spending a lot of time with another man or woman, it's a small community and tongues start wagging. It's a tension, especially for the younger women," she says. "No one talks about it because you don't want to make people uncomfortable."

Other times, a nice guy overcompensates, nattering at length about his wife and children so the woman across the table knows he's not pulling any funny stuff. "I had a meeting with someone I view as a mentor, and the whole time we were talking he was trying to balance his values. He was talking about his wife, trying to establish right out of the gate that he was aboveboard," says Lili Balfour, the founder of Atelier Advisors, a boutique investment bank. "The same thing happened to a female client of mine who was worried about having a one-on-one meeting with a male investor. But he kept talking about his wife and kids to make sure she knew it was clear. It's smart for men to bring another female or lay it out right away."

And what about men who treat a woman *too* much like one of the guys? Well, that can backfire too, as when Balfour spent a few painful hours with a client who bragged about dating a twenty-year-old waitress. "I just thought, 'What a douche bag,'" she laughs.

"You don't want to create animosity or make people uncomfortable. Men who have integrity will be more on guard, whereas others will say, 'Well, screw these women.' It's a delicate issue."

It's a delicate issue because it's real. Diversity is grand and liberation is divine, but "Let's Get It On" still trumps "Free to Be You and Me" at most big firms. Companies screen for people who fit their culture and share the same values. They hunt for employees with chemistry, just not too much. It's in a firm's interest to ensure that networking between the sexes includes no actual sex, that rubbing is confined to elbows. But just like that federal judge met her husband in her courtroom (Chapter 2), and just like Kim Moses found the man of her life in the office across the hall, things happen. People fall in love.

These issues have always existed, but somehow they're less threatening when there's real sympathy between men and women—when Mars and Venus know that while their orbits diverge, they're still circling the same sun.

In this swelling universe, Stiletto Networks exert their own gravitational pull. Where ladies used to hide their groups, now they're loud and proud. The tenor of their dialogue has shifted; it's lost that garish martyrdom, the frothing rancor and melancholic air of consciousness-raising that made highfliers wince. These gals are no longer trading war stories about hiding breast pumps or being directed to the service entrance at private men's clubs. Instead of lamenting 77 cents on the dollar, they have their eyes on the prize.

Women are quick to reassure male colleagues that their clusters are not "wine and bitch" sessions. "It's either personal, work/life balance stuff like 'How do you juggle traveling with kids? Should I get the night nurse?'" says Theresia Gouw Ranzetta, who is in her early forties and married with two young children. "Or it's business: 'Are you looking for someone to run marketing? I think I know someone who embodies that brand.'"

As the female slant matures, male perceptions change too—and with them, the "comfort formula." Men now view women's groups as reservoirs of talent rather than receptacles of resentment. "It used to be that we would get together and network, but we felt we shouldn't let guys know because they might think we're complaining about men. But now it's the opposite. It's gone from something we did in stealth to something we're proud of," Ranzetta continues. "My partners see the power of these women's networking events. The guys want us to get access now because it opens up a new channel for our executives. They're thankful I invite our female founders to these things because it increases visibility for the companies. There's an understanding that we're not there bitching. We're just trying to get stuff done for the companies."

THE STILETTO NETWORK REVOLUTION

Women's networks are becoming prestigious because they enable gals to do what guys have done since time immemorial: capitalize on connections. Without warning, Stiletto Networks are "coming out of the closet" as members execute high-profile, high-stakes transactions together.

But many women insist their networks are the result of evolution, not revolution. These groups formed over time as more women climbed corporate ladders and sought like-minded friends. Now, forty years later, there are finally enough accomplished ladies in the workforce to impact each other's careers and to grease the wheels for talented up-and-comers. It's a natural progression, not a movement, they say. Women are simply coming of age in all spheres.

"There's a reason this is happening now, and it's a Catch-22 when I bring it up," says Heidi Roizen. "It's because women have finally achieved a critical mass in certain areas. There are now more qualified women to do the work." Roizen claims she doesn't intentionally mastermind megadeals among her female compatriots—

even among her "Fave 5"—and it's not like she woke up one day and realized there's an unexploited niche called "high-quality women." But, more and more, she's doing business with the girls.

> *Networking isn't a zero-sum game; it's just good business and good karma to assist qualified people.*

"At the end of the day, a lot of women say it's about the quality of my life. I can define happiness in four words: meaningful work, meaningful relationships," she continues. "There is something special when you hang out with another woman who is facing some of the challenges and successes you are, especially when it's over a glass of wine. Sometimes it's sharing a laugh, sometimes a knowing nod. Many women bond over the juggle when it comes to home life. At the end of the day you're still a mom, and by and large most men don't deal with that the way women do, regardless of anyone's position. It isn't about equality movements; it's about common ground and shared experiences that increase our ability to trust each other. You realize you can help each other out."

When Roizen aids another woman professionally, she doesn't necessarily expect payback. Networking isn't a zero-sum game; it's just good business and good karma to assist qualified people. "I don't do it with the idea that I'm putting a dollar in the relationship bank that I'll withdraw someday. It's because I enjoy associating with talented women across an age spectrum. I do it because it feels right," she says. "There's a certain comfort level when—even if the person is in a different field—they've achieved an equivalent level of success. The best groups I've participated in have been small and ad hoc, six women saying, 'Let's go away together for the weekend to have a lot of fun and get some work done as well.'"

While these women are capable and confident operating in male-dominated environments, they enjoy working with people they identify with in a more intimate way, in a manner that merges business and friendship. "I'm a social person, so I tend to develop closer relationships with my business colleagues," Dana Evan of Babes in Boyland says. "Business is personal. When I think back to my business relationships, either with customers or peers, they're all personal at the end of the day. That's one of the reasons networking works. It's not something new, but I think as more and more women are put in executive positions, this interaction is elevated."

The Quilting Bee Transferred to the Boardroom

Stiletto Networks emerge because their members find fast affinities. Women's ways of bonding and communicating have always been different from men's, so maybe the ladies are finally at ease acknowledging and accentuating these differences, integrating all sundry parts of themselves into the boardroom. Sure, women talk about transactions, but they also do girly things like hosting baby showers and swapping Manolos. Where men might fall back on sports, women use clothes and shoes as an icebreaker, the initial step to a more substantive relationship. "It's okay to compliment another woman on her dress or shoes," Roizen laughs. "Just because you admire what's happening on the outside doesn't mean you're not interested in what's going on inside her head."

Since the beginning of time, women have come together to talk, cook, tell stories, and seek advice. Networks—be they the car pool, the PTA, or the Girl Scouts—have always been important to women, and Stiletto Networks are a natural extension. Stiletto Networks employ the same skills women have always brought to bear in their endeavors: a collaborative spirit ("I'll pick up the kids

Monday if you do it Thursday," "I'll watch your kids while you make dinner"), trust and empathy ("I'll bring your family dinner every night when you're sick, and I know you'll do the same for me"), and an ability to maximize scarce resources ("I'll find a way to feed five children with these two potatoes"). The means are the same, but the venue is new. These ladies' talents, honed over generations, are now being unleashed on a larger stage—the business world—for maximum impact. *It's the quilting bee transferred to the boardroom.*

But there's a revolution happening too.

Recent years have seen an eruption of Stiletto Networks, which now exist among women at every level, from CEOs to middle managers to twenty-something entrepreneurs to moms launching businesses in their basements. Each group might have as few as five women, but in aggregate they total in the tens if not hundreds of thousands of women nationwide. Yet it's not just this uptick in number that's significant. Other forces are conspiring to lift the profile of Stiletto Networks, making them powerful and effective, and changing the way work is accomplished in the twenty-first century.

No one would deny that technology has transformed the workplace. Gadgets, mobility, and changing work patterns enable people to surface new partners and friends and to maintain broader and stronger relationships than were ever possible before. Telephone time has decreased and become more efficient, and relationships maps, as facilitated by Facebook and LinkedIn, now resemble interrelated starbursts. Finding the world's preeminent expert in anything—from the orthopedist to fix your bum knee to the designer to create a visual identity for your brand—requires surprisingly little effort.

How does this relate to women? Women have always reached out more broadly, and today's tools allow them to extend their tentacles even further. When women can quickly look online to see what their friends and coworkers are up to, it's easy to do more of what comes naturally: making connections, be they in the PTA or for professional advancement.

"Tech is enabling and facilitating the ability to reach across different pools of relationships, across different shared interests and needs. We are able to maintain very active relationships," Roizen says. "Twenty or thirty years ago, you defined yourself by the connections you could create and maintain, but they were narrower. Now I can meet women who have similar experiences in the workplace. I can augment face-to-face relationships and affiliate and identify myself as part of networks that don't require my physical proximity. And I can maintain those ties without being physically present."

Women's virtual networks are a straightforward extension of their offline friendships and, both on- and offline, women are more active than men. As Aileen Lee, a partner at Kleiner Perkins, points out in "Why Women Rule the Internet," her popular post on TechCrunch.com from March 2011, studies by Pew, Quantcast, Nielsen, and comScore all show that women have flocked to social networking sites. Nielsen says women are responsible for 55 percent of mobile social network usage and, according to comScore, women spend more time online, including 30 percent more time social networking than men.

Women are a majority of Facebook's 1 billion users. Sheryl Sandberg has said that women embraced the site first, joining groups and uploading pictures, and that they have 8 percent more "friends" on average than men. Women drive 71 percent of daily fan activity on Facebook and are responsible for 62 percent of status updates, messages, and comments. On Twitter, almost two-thirds of shares and retweets are by women; women follow more people, and are followed more than men, even when numbers are adjusted for celebrities. Not to mention Groupon, where 77 percent of deal seekers are female.

Given the mingling-on-steroids the Web has enabled, it matters less that there are fewer women in any one company or profession. Women don't have to—as Kelly Williams of Credit Suisse said—rely on bumping into other accomplished ladies in the hallway. When they want to find friends or experts, they hop online. And while true trust in business still stems from meaningful, often face-to-face exchanges over time, technology lubricates these interactions. Technology fast-forwards the cross-industry, horizontal networks women have been forging all along.

Funny enough, because of their increasingly powerful Stiletto Networks, women are now more likely to run into each other in the hallways of major corporations too. Stiletto Networks are responsible for propelling women not only up the company ladder but also from firm to firm, industry to industry.

The days of "company men" are over, and employees of both genders job-hop. Now, a chief marketing officer might leave a retail chain to work at a global media company before launching her own social media start-up. This cross-pollination smudges the lines. Industries overlap and are interdependent in ways that were inconceivable a decade ago, and workers can no longer afford to stay stuck in a particular silo, oblivious to developments in other fields.

> By helping and hiring each other, women find the allies they were missing before. They acquire a stronger collective voice within their companies.

Stiletto Networks facilitate these moves for women. It's easier to gather intelligence and leapfrog when you have relationships with senior executives in other functions. A woman can now legitimately recommend a smart, qualified member of her Stiletto Network who has worked in another industry for a job in her own firm. Where once they knew each other only socially, now they become aligned professionally as well. By helping and hiring each other, women find the allies they were missing before. They acquire a stronger collective voice within their companies.

Of course, cross-pollination isn't confined to women, but women have a head start. What began as a negative—the search for friends and allies outside their industries because they couldn't find them internally—has become a strategic advantage, as both established firms and start-ups strive for global, wide-ranging insight.

Companies of all sizes are mixing and matching to stay competitive. They too have realized that when people from different backgrounds compare notes and brainstorm, advances occur. Even blue-chip behemoths are trying to capitalize on these junctions, hiring more contract workers and encouraging employees to team up on "big-picture" projects that span departments. In the new economy, the ability to draw knowledge from diverse spheres is prized. Horizontal networks are a boon.

"Top performers have networks with more bridging ties," says Robert Cross, an associate professor of management at the University of Virginia and research director of the Network Roundtable, a consortium of seventy-five organizations sponsoring research on network applications to critical management issues. Cross takes an analytical, data-driven approach to measuring collaboration inside name-brand, international firms, mapping interactions that generate revenue.

Insularity, Cross says, is a great hindrance to career progression. Most leaders, even when they rise within a company, continue to maintain 60 to 70 percent of their strongest ties to employees from their original business units. This unduly influences decisions, as they continue to view the whole organization from the perspective of a single department. People with insular networks become closed off from opportunities; they might not hear about a deal or have access to the colleague who could help sell or deliver a new product.

According to Cross, people generally surround themselves with those who look and think in similar ways. But employees who quickly learn to acquire new expertise or supplement skill gaps are much more likely to succeed. "It sounds obvious, but it's very common. People keep turning back to their existing circle of friends. Almost all of us have three to five people we rely on for way too much; we keep going back to someone who might not be the right expert at the right time. We mistake trust or liking as real expertise," he says. "When you have a disproportionate influence, when you constantly rely on people in the area you came from for help and advice, it creates an invisible anchor. There's a higher likelihood of getting blindsided because you're not fully aware of what's happening out there and operating on it."

Top performers, however, reach across functional lines, building relationships and gathering intelligence from a range of departments. Because they don't let the same colleagues get scheduled around them, they're able to see their original business unit in perspective. They gain a balanced view of the company as a whole.

Cross doesn't specifically focus on gender, and he says that networks of successful men and women look quite similar. Both high-performing men and women are able to obtain political and personal support, as well as developmental feedback. Still, certain differences have become apparent over time.

Men develop task-based networks; they focus on the activity at hand and don't spend as much time building trust with coworkers. But, Cross points out, trust seldom begins with tasks. While trust is critical to most jobs, it almost always begins in off-task conversations that show people have the same values and care about the same things. "Men don't do that well. Often when I'm doing executive coaching, that's the one area I'm always pushing on. Sometimes it's better to leave the task on the table and build the relationship," Cross says. "The relationship will bring more to you over time because the other person trusts you and is energized by where you're going."

Women, however, do this naturally. Remember all that prattle about clothes and shoes? The bonding over the struggles of family life? Turns out it's not just idle chitchat. It's about building trust, and it's a plus for women in the workplace.

"Men home in on one or two other people, whereas women tend to source things from a broader range of people. Women use networks in a way that brings balance into their lives—education, hobbies, spiritual things like religion or yoga. These are ways to get reenergized, to find balance and a sense of purpose. It might be a more sustainable approach to handling life today, because if men lose a job or a spouse, there's nothing else there," Cross continues.

"One of the things that really matters is having people around you who give you a sense of purpose. If people do that well, they seem to be able to rise and be successful over time without suffering burnout. We know that broader nontask-related networks lead to more resilient leaders and people who handle stress better. It may be an advantage for women today. Especially if things are happening as a result and money is flowing, I completely agree with the power of these networks."

Innovation Junction

Money *is* flowing, and things—including job creation—are happening as a result of Stiletto Networks. Creativity emerges from this mash-up of skills, and innovation occurs at the intersection of disciplines and value-creation streams. Original products and ventures are forming.

Even ten years ago, if you were a senior executive in technology and your best friend worked in retail, you never expected to do enormous deals together. You never thought to partner and launch new companies. But today firms like Gilt Groupe are thriving. Gilt is an amalgam of technology, media, fashion, homeware, food, and travel, and the company relies on partnerships with firms in each of these fields.

"You figure out what you have to trade when you're short on capital," says Susan Lyne of Gilt Groupe over breakfast at Sarabeth's, near her home in Manhattan's Carnegie Hill neighborhood. "We offered to do a private sale for Starbucks' best customers because we had more advanced targeting capabilities. We got 25,000 to 35,000 new customers because Starbucks didn't have a way to target smaller groups online. With Target, we knew they had fashion-conscious customers who loved their designer collaborations, so we partnered on a sale to reach that audience.

"The world is changing so quickly," continues Lyne, who is also on the board of AOL. "The first employee of Gilt was hired five years ago. If you look back five years, a year after Facebook opened up to more than just the college market, Twitter was just an idea, Foursquare didn't exist, iPads and netbooks hadn't launched. The whole app-based Internet browsing experience had yet to emerge. Think of the number of businesses built on these trends. These horizontal relationships, the cross-fertilization and connections, have generated ideas for new businesses."

In addition to attending banker Nancy Peretsman's girl gatherings, Lyne has been a guest at The Vault, Kim Moses's group in L.A. Lyne has experience with women across a wide range of industries and has witnessed the power of Stiletto Networks firsthand. "These women are providing business intel for each other. Unless you have people willing to share points of view, you'll get lost," Lyne says. "It helps provide a snapshot for where the world is heading. We're ready for it, we know how to take advantage of it."

Women are relying on Stiletto Networks more than ever in the current recession, when companies must be nimble and creative to compete. "I believe strongly that in this postrecession world, successful companies are able to adapt and evolve," says Sara Holoubek, whose consulting firm, Luminary Labs, works primarily with industries undergoing massive transformation, such as healthcare, automotive, and education. "Our clients are not buying a widget. They seek to become more agile and therefore more resilient in the face of change. It's like an organism that contracts and expands as needed and is not constrained by a framework. You don't have to do things the way they were done before. Businesses still running that way are failing."

Companies are expected to turn on a dime, to respond in real time to the market's demands, and increasingly Holoubek advises clients to operate on a networked business model including contract employees. These part-timers are everywhere. In the past few years, more than 5 million people have been unemployed long term and more than 8 million are working part-time because they can't find steady jobs. Some will be first in line once full-time positions are created. Others no longer want to return to structured employment after they've tasted the freedom that project-based work allows. They're happy to land stints as consultants or advisers working on mission-driven teams. And then there's the eager swarm of Baby Boomers who will not go gentle into that good night. They're aging out of their first careers, but rejecting the golf course. Collaborating on projects is a way to earn extra money and keep their minds engaged, yet still have more flexibility than the traditional workday permits.

Contract workers are busy stitching patchwork careers. Just as in Silicon Valley, they depend on their networks for opportunities, and Holoubek draws from this vast pool to run her own business. In addition to full-time staff, Luminary Labs leverages "luminaries at large," subject experts who either consult long term or swoop in on a project-by-project basis depending on clients' needs. They're not freelancers, Holoubek says, but rather a SWAT team of independent consultants and small businesses, "an integral part of the twenty-first-century workforce, weaving in and out to provide optimal value." As a result, Holoubek can pursue an array of engagements, provided she knows the right people to tap.

So far, this model is working. Holoubek set a revenue target of $1 million in 2010, the firm's first year, and achieved it in the first quarter. In 2011, revenue more than doubled over the previous year, and in 2012, revenue is projected to more than double again. Luminary Labs has been consistently profitable in the recession.

> *"The world is changing so quickly. These horizontal relationships, the cross-fertilization connections, have generated ideas for new businesses." —Susan Lyne*

Holoubek finds that 80 percent of the fifty consultants employed by Luminary Labs are women, an inadvertent development. Holoubek—who is in her late thirties, married to an opera singer, and just had her first child—didn't set out to have a majority-female firm. But, she says, more women seem attracted to flexibility—or, perhaps, comfortable with instability. So, she wonders, are women inherently more amenable to a business model she believes is the wave of the future?

"Historically, women have on-ramped and off-ramped. They've had to make these decisions when they've had children. They've stepped away and managed transitions and then relied on their networks to get back in. Because of this, we're more accustomed to a networked model. It may take men longer to catch up, just as it's taking women longer to catch up in building net worth," Holoubek says. "These networks can be leveraged in incredible ways. My hypothesis is that if women are comfortable in networks—talking about everything from where they got their hair cut to what they invest in—that's a real advantage."

Collaboration and Authenticity

At least in part because of the Great Recession, a new management style is also taking root—one that is flat and nonhierarchical and integrates input from many different sources. "The nature of work is much more about collaboration than it's ever been in the past. Younger companies have to outsource and partner because they don't have the resources to do everything in-house. And major corporations are sticking to their core businesses and outsourcing noncore activities," says Connie Duckworth, the founder and CEO of ARZU, Inc., a social business enterprise working in Afghanistan, who was also the first female sales and trading partner in the history of Goldman Sachs. "In virtually every field, there are fewer and fewer silos, so by definition the work and leadership is multidisciplinary. That's another reason you need to collaborate and have diverse networks. Each trend contributes to and accelerates the others."

Duckworth, who is on the board of the NorthShore University HealthSystem in Evanston, Illinois, uses medical research as an example. "NIH used to fund in a siloed way, but that's not so anymore," she says of the National Institutes of Health, the world's largest source of funding for medical research. "Medical research by definition is being driven to be multidisciplinary because there's more understanding of the nature, origin, and impact of disease. That's how research is being conducted, and that's how NIH is choosing to fund research these days. They're forcing collaboration."

Historically and stereotypically, this is how women prefer to work. "The skills needed in this more conceptual economy are the things women are very good at—dealing with things that are murky, not black and white, that require judgment and intuition," says Deborah Wince-Smith, the president and CEO of the Council on Competitiveness, a coalition of CEOs, labor leaders, and university presidents working together to help Americans prosper. Wince-Smith's own career has zigged and zagged, which she says has worked to her benefit. She was a classical Bronze Age archaeologist who then managed an exchange program between American and Eastern European scientists for the National Science Foundation. Wince-Smith also worked in the Reagan administration, overseeing international science and technology cooperation with strategic partners like Japan, China, India, and Russia, and later served as the first assistant secretary of commerce for technology policy in the administration of President George H. W. Bush.

Looking back, she attributes her success to an ability to make correlations across multiple disciplines. "When I first started my career, I felt I was at a disadvantage because I didn't have a PhD in science. But many scientists didn't think across sectors; they thought narrowly in their stovepipes," says Wince-Smith, who is also a Senate-confirmed member of the IRS Oversight Board and a former board member of NASDAQ OMX. "I learned quickly for the work I was doing that I needed to connect the dots, look at interconnections between things and elucidate their import. You need to have a much broader approach to thinking and innovation to create the breakthrough, game-changing products and services of our time, and women are very skilled at that. We're synthetic, as opposed to linear, thinkers."

The term *authentic leadership* also gets a lot of buzz these days. As many managers admit, it's easy to be phony when the money's flowing. Companies can bestow generous bonuses, throw parties, or supply coffee and pastries at meetings. These perks can disguise a dysfunctional working environment, but during a downturn it's harder to put lipstick on a pig.

"During a downturn, you have to do the most with other resources you have. You have to say, 'We don't have the ability to add headcount,' and motivate people to work harder for less. You have to tap into your network," Sara Holoubek says. "In a downturn, you see people become very real and, if they're good, come up with creative solutions. That authenticity is appreciated."

A hierarchical, militaristic approach no longer applies, and business leaders have been forced to adapt to this matrix environment. The horizontal networks women have built over time just happen to be the same networks society now wants and needs. Women's flat, cross-sector groups are poised to solve today's complex problems, to advance the economy, and to propel civilization forward.

"We're moving away from the corporate model. We're coming into an era where women have the skill sets and core value systems. Being collegial, collaborative, checking your ego at the door, and trying to work on solutions. Being able to work in a nonhierarchical environment, listening, attuned to intuition. These are increasingly all characteristics of senior leaders," says Catherine Allen, CEO of the Santa Fe Group, a strategic consulting firm, who was also the founding CEO of the financial industry consortium BITS. Allen worked closely with the U.S. Treasury and the Department of Homeland Security and became the coordination point to protect the nation's financial services system after the terrorist attacks of September 11, 2001.

"Women intuitively understand this. We have that capacity, as mothers and sisters and preservers of the family," Allen asserts. "When we come through this period, I think we'll find many more women at the senior level."

The Money Trail

Another sign Stiletto Networks are gaining clout? New businesses are cropping up to serve them. There is money to be made from groups whose members have influence, independence, and spending power.

Lisbeth McNabb, the former CFO of the dating site Match.com, founded w2wlink.com to unite professional women across industries and geographies and to help women advance their careers. "I saw a convergence in the marketplace of business associations for women. Right now, there are so many women in transition and pursuing goals, women who need inspiration and solutions," says McNabb, who is in her early fifties and has led high-growth business units in many different industries, including media, telecom, banking, and airlines. "I realized that part of what had been happening offline could be replicated online with greater efficiency."

Her site targets college-educated women, particularly between ages 35 and 45, who are either entrepreneurs or on the corporate fast track, and particularly those dissatisfied in their current jobs.

These ladies have hit a "pain point" and are looking for guidance, or they're in transition and trying to determine the next step. Perhaps they're considering a new position or are experiencing health problems, a divorce, or the birth of a child.

McNabb says she's leading the "professional women's space," reaching more than 20,000 free and paid subscribers and claiming more than 2 million monthly engagement points with the site, meaning that women are reading articles published by w2wlink.com through Facebook, LinkedIn, and push e-mails. McNabb launched a complementary site in India and has teamed up with ClubCorp to host in-person events in at least eight cities for w2wlink.com members and affiliates. She has also partnered with large companies like PepsiCo, American Airlines, and PricewaterhouseCoopers, which include w2wlink.com on their internal sites to show commitment to female employees. PwC uses the site to keep alumnae in the loop as well; if a woman has left to raise young children or care for aging parents, she remains in the company's network and is encouraged to return to work full- or part-time as soon as she's able.

"Times of transition force people to look around. The negative becomes a positive," says McNabb, who hosts monthly salons in her Dallas home and is on the board of Astia, an investment vehicle for female entrepreneurs. "There are a lot of women who are not natural connectors, but once they've had a disruption, they learn the importance of being more collaborative."

McNabb isn't alone in trying to profit from an emergent channel of female executives. Patricia Lizarraga, the former managing director of Credit Agricole Securities' New York mergers and acquisitions group, founded Hypatia Capital, a New York–based private equity firm and merchant bank that sources deals from and for top female executives at Fortune 1000 companies. Lizarraga is generating proprietary deal flow by building relationships with female executives interested in acquiring midsize businesses. Through search firms, referrals, and direct marketing, and by hosting invitation-only "CEO Roadmap" seminars that provide an insider view of private equity, she has built a network of 4,000 senior managers and board members, including more than 150 at the CEO level.

Lizarraga says executive women often leave organizations when they're passed over for promotion, or when they realize they lack sponsors to lift them to the C-suite. These ladies are experienced leaders of massive business units, well qualified to lead portfolio companies—which Lizarraga presents as a viable option if they hit corporate glass ceilings.

> "If you run a huge business unit, don't go be an entrepreneur. Buy a company. My pitch to all my potential CEOs is to go bigger."—Patricia Lizarraga

"You see a lot of very senior women become entrepreneurs, but they go and do small things. These women max out in their firms and then go start some very small company. You ran a $500 million business, so why do you want to run a $5 million business? If you run a huge business unit, don't go be an entrepreneur. Buy a company," she says. "My pitch to all my potential CEOs is to go bigger. The bigger the company you manage, the more you control your time. Most senior women are mothers and married, so they're great at time management, and part of what I'm trying to share is that it's not necessary for you to dial back."

Lizarraga sees these executives as an untapped segment, and she hopes to capitalize on her first-mover advantage in harnessing female talent. And, she says, her business is a blast. Lizarraga loves meeting engaging, inspiring achievers, and by the third conversation she finds they're talking at all levels, sharing details of their home lives. She says women divulge all sorts of industry intelligence to her and, almost without exception, Lizarraga's potential CEOs have given her their personal e-mail addresses. She relates to them, and she is building both professional and personal relationships she hopes to monetize over time.

"We're here to make money. I'm making my business network female because I think it's an unexploited niche by other bankers who happen to be guys," she says. "Most of the women I'm contacting have very limited contact with private equity. That forty-five-year-old guy might feel uncomfortable or even intimidated by a senior, more accomplished woman CEO. He has no connection. But I talk to [these women], and they want to talk to me because they know I'm not inviting them to coffee to talk about childcare. I'm bringing them deals that will make them millions. Guys could have called these women, but they didn't."

Like Sara Holoubek, Lizarraga, who is in her mid-forties and has a young daughter, is building a network-based business that capitalizes on women's desire for flexibility. Hypatia has eight managing directors, seven of whom are female, and Lizarraga gives them ultimate control of their time. They can work from home, from Starbucks, or from Hypatia's midtown Manhattan office. They can tackle as many deals as they want. They can use Hypatia's Rolodex or their own. But here's the hitch: No one gets paid until the deal closes.

"There's obviously a bigger risk than if you're working in a bank, but I am confident in this model. Men don't see themselves doing anything but working. We're constantly thinking, 'Am I in or am I out?'" Lizarraga explains. "My idea for Hypatia has always been that the world cannot expect women to fit into the workplace. The workplace has to find a way to accommodate women. Research tells us that women value flexibility over money. For entrepreneurs, that's possible, but entrepreneurs are only a small percentage of the population. Most people need a much more stable life. The workplace as it's structured today doesn't accommodate that."

Limited partners initially warned her that only 14 percent of senior executives are female, which means there just aren't enough women qualified to lead companies. But nearly 73 percent of Fortune 500 companies have at least one female executive officer. And Lizzaraga contends that 14 percent of every Fortune 1000 company, plus 14 percent of the next 1,000 companies, actually encompass an eye-popping number of potential female CEOs. "When I started this business five years ago, I read every bio of every single female executive in the Fortune 1000," she says. "I know what these women can do."

Still, by Lizarraga's own assessment, Hypatia is not yet a success. The firm is profitable and can handily execute a $100 million deal, but has yet to complete the landmark $1 billion deal. "Relationships are monetized over ten- to twenty-year periods, not two-year periods. Periodicity on the banking side is very low, and you can't make transactions happen because they're strategic in nature. How often do you sell your company, once or twice in your life?" she asks. "We've done some small stuff, but we need to get something big and high-profile. We still need one really big, visible deal."

Even with these qualifiers, Lizarraga says it's only a matter of time. "There are more women in powerful or semi-powerful positions. Women have reached achievement, but not leadership, so we're still trying on a lot of these roles," she says. "This is a huge trend. It's happening informally, and I'm trying to capitalize on it formally. It's still new, but there will be a money trail."

WALK THE TALK

ike kids on a road trip, women can't seem to stop asking: "Are we there yet?" Inevitably, the answer is no.

While the rest of the nation nurses saplings, Silicon Valley points to sequoias. But even there, not everyone's a believer. "On the West Coast we have the mythology of the meritocracy," says Sharon Vosmek, the CEO of Astia, a nonprofit that provides seed capital for female entrepreneurs. "The stronger the notion of meritocracy, the more difficult it is for women. If everyone's telling me it's a meritocracy and I'm feeling it's harder for me than the guy next to me, I'll internalize that. I'll think it's about me. Meritocracy is absolutely our goal, but we haven't yet achieved it."

Vosmek, whose background is in public policy and who studied women's participation in markets, says that historically the hurdles have been higher for women because they've lacked access to male business networks. "It's absolutely about relationships, and there are hidden biases. The little data we have shows that even where we think we don't have a bias, we still do where it relates to leadership."

She cites a Harvard Business School case study on Heidi Roizen that was distributed to students in an organizational behavior class at Columbia Business School. In an effort to test gender stereotypes, professors changed Heidi's name to "Howard" in half the cases. Then they asked students to evaluate the central character based on traits like ambition, generosity, and concern for others. When students believed the protagonist was a woman, they judged her an aggressive, power-hungry self-promoter, whereas "Howard" was someone they'd take out for a beer.

Vosmek also says that when Stanford University wrote Astia's first business case, the nonprofit learned that it was viewed as substandard solely because it focused on women. "Women are half the population, half the PhDs, half the MBAs, 70 percent of last year's valedictorians," she proclaims. "There is no sound reason we should be only 7 percent of venture investment. But on the venture side, 98 percent of the participants are men and 90 percent of angel investors are men. So how do you expose women to the opportunity and convince them they have the skills to pursue it?"

Astia is doing its part, cultivating investors, a board, and an adviser network that is half male. "We want to be inclusive, not create a women's network," Vosmek says. "That's the next generation of business, so the networks we build must have equal representation. It creates a very different vibe when you hit that ratio. It's innovative, but it doesn't make everyone uncomfortable."

Indians Do It Better

Until full assimilation occurs, Vosmek wishes more women would act like Indians.

In 1992, a group of male Silicon Valley executives with roots in the Indus region realized they were being treated like second-class citizens. They created the first chapter of The Indus Entrepreneurs (TiE). "We had foreign accents, different educations and values. We dressed differently. People thought, 'I can't put this guy in front of a client, I can't invest in this guy's company,'" says Vivek Wadhwa, a serial entrepreneur and academic who founded the Carolinas chapter of TiE. "We couldn't pretend there wasn't a problem."

Members of TiE systematically sponsored and invested in each other. Each prosperous Indian found a promising protégé to groom. The mentor did whatever was necessary—from making introductions to personally funding to buying new clothes—to help the greenhorn adapt and achieve. The members aimed, as TiE's website says, to foster a "virtuous cycle of wealth creation and giving back to the community." TiE now has about 13,000 members in sixty-one chapters across seventeen countries and, as a result, Wadhwa says Southeast Asians have become a disproportionately successful, sought-out bloc in the workforce.

"It worked for us because we banded together. We fixed the problem systematically and led by example," he says. "Women fit into society better because you're only different in one sense. It's easier for you to pretend you're the same as guys, but you need to recognize there's still a problem."

> *Ladies need to overcome the risk aversion that defines so many; they need to ask for what they're worth and lay their money down.*

Even the white boys agree. Steve Blank, a serial entrepreneur who has taught at the University of California at Berkeley, Stanford, and Columbia, says that Silicon Valley in the late 1970s was a sea of homogeny. "The notion of Chinese or Indians running a company was laughable. They were good engineers, but couldn't run a company," says Blank, who was listed as one of *Harvard Business Review*'s "Masters of Innovation" in 2012. "Over the last thirty years, almost every ethnicity started a support group. People collect over the notion of tribes, and the women-thing is the next rational barrier to fall. I have two college-age daughters, and it's time."

All hail the diaspora! But let's not forget when we talk about TiE, we talk about guys. Women have their own distinct issues, and groups of girls gabbing are not going to jump-start a cultural revolution. Ladies need to overcome the risk aversion that defines so many; they need to ask for what they're worth and lay their money down. "How many women are raising $500,000 when they should be raising $5 million? They think they're not qualified and downplay their skills," Sharon Vosmek asserts. "I saw a woman who ran a successful hedge fund for fifteen years underestimate herself at a meeting. When asked the market for her company, she admitted it was five times what she'd stated in a presentation, but she didn't want to be held to that. We need to get women to think of and promote themselves as experts."

Maria Cirino, a former serial entrepreneur with four winning exits and the cofounder of .406 Ventures, a venture capital firm in Boston, says many of the women she meets lack confidence. "Women say, 'I'd love to discuss an idea with you' or 'I want to get advice, but I'm not here for money,' as if their silly little businesses can't be worth someone else's money," says Cirino, whose company got its name from the unsurpassed .406 batting average that Ted Williams posted for the Boston Red Sox in 1941. "Whereas guys strut in and they're shocked when they don't walk out with a check, like it's their God-given right to get money for their ideas."

For a host of reasons, from hormones to societal conditioning, women are more cautious. When men eye a worthy investment, they ask their buddies to pony up. "They have $10 million before they blink an eye, and that gives them credibility when they approach the institutional folks," says another female VC. "If women think an investment is a good idea, they say, 'First present to me, then to my husband, then to my wealth adviser.' And then, if they do invest, it's half or less than a guy who'd talked to you for forty-five minutes."

This VC likens it to auctions, where men outbid each other in testosterone-fueled duels while women sit on their hands and gawk. Or, she says, it's like that scene in the film *Reds*, where Warren Beatty chastises a friend for excluding him from some risky deal. "I saw that movie recently and I turned to my husband and said, 'That is just *not* something a woman would do.'"

Sharon Vosmek sees a valuable informal network of female executives and investors emerging now, just in the last few years. "When there's actual money being made by women and invested in women, you're going to see more and more. VC firms with women in the partnership are 70 percent more likely to have a woman founder in their portfolios," she says. "I do think there's a new network emerging, but it feels like eucalyptus trees. They grow tall and fast, but they don't have deep roots."

Could this be the beginning of the roots? Taking the tree analogy one step further, Vosmek says yes. As Stiletto Networks become more prevalent, they create the affirmative access and opportunity women were lacking in the past. "Maybe we're becoming redwoods. Redwoods cluster and grow multiple trees out of the same root bed, and the roots go way down," Vosmek continues. "Women become redwoods through collaborative effort. It's when all these disparate approaches come together that we achieve."

Mentor's Walks

If women need to stand together, then why are they retreating home? Don't these little dinner groups smack of Tupperware parties, with ladies shrinking from the world and taking shelter in their kitchens? And how about that element of masturbatory self-validation? It's easy to feel superior when entrenched among needy disciples, when everyone looks and sounds just like you.

Shouldn't women be strutting their stuff on rostrums, staging events and declaring their authority, flaunting their strength in numbers? Whatever happened to the rallying cry?

The rallying cry, it turns out, falls on deaf ears. And it's resulted in a lot of hoarse voices. Conferences, with their eternal blend of backslapping and ass kissing and chest pounding at the dais, haven't much worked for women. Ballrooms only count if they pave the way to boardrooms, and that just hasn't happened.

Most women say that unless they're being honored or featured as panelists, these gatherings are an unmitigated snooze. Halls fill quickly with consultants and insurance executives trolling for new clients, and women rarely meet the people they need to meet. These ladies are already short on time, and they're striving to build real and valuable bonds with people who will go the distance. "At Allen they say, 'Why don't you have a women's conference?'" says Nancy Peretsman, the prominent banker. "Well, the world doesn't need another large women's conference. My question is: Are these people who would go to your funeral?"

Faced with one more rubber-chicken meal, women say they'd rather chill with their friends. Or with friends of friends. Or with any crowd that applies a strict filter for character, aptitude, and experience.

In this era of content overload, seeds of intimacy aren't sown at mass-produced dinners where speakers serve the same hackneyed lines. Women can't leave relationship building to party planners. Faced with one more rubber-chicken meal, women say they'd rather chill with their friends. Or with friends of friends. Or with any crowd that applies a strict filter for character, aptitude, and experience. Dinners at homes or in quiet restaurants involve less pantomime and pageantry, but more intimacy. And more intimacy leads to more loyalty. And more loyalty leads to a true desire to extend oneself for others.

As a result, this riptide of small, interlocking, homey circles is shaking the foundation in ways women's conferences never could. For women, home is where the heart is. And heart is where the power is. And power just might lead to that brass ring of equality.

And, though it might sound counterintuitive, women are also taking it to the streets. No, they're not storming the barricades, just enjoying a leisurely promenade in their sweats. In the course of toning their bodies, they're also expanding minds—and maybe, just maybe, changing the world.

Geraldine Laybourne, the iconic Nickelodeon executive who founded Oxygen Media, the only female-owned and -operated cable network, has been walking with women for years and hatching big plans. It all started in the 1970s, when Laybourne was leading a children's television production company and found herself "lifted up" by another woman, Bernice Coe. Coe had been raised in a very poor section of Newark, New Jersey, but she'd managed to attend Vassar College and earn a master's degree from Columbia. She spent twenty years making educational films before founding Coe Film Associates, which supplied programs by independent filmmakers to cable television networks, including Nickelodeon, HBO, Showtime, the

Discovery Channel, A&E, and the Disney Channel. "She was a very self-starting, brilliant person," Laybourne says. "And she decided the cable TV industry was going to be good for other women."

Coe introduced Laybourne's production company to Nickelodeon, the then-fledgling children's network, where Laybourne soon went in-house. And Coe kept following up, calling Laybourne with names of other women she should meet. "Just one woman got me my job at Nickelodeon. She followed us, she hemmed our pants, she took me to my first foreign festival, she gave us notes on our speeches. She would sit in the front row and smile. Anne Sweeney was one of her people, and I was one," Laybourne continues, referring to the co-chair of Disney Media Networks and the president of Disney/ABC Television Group. "[Coe] said, 'We're going to be our own group,' and we decided we were going to help other women. We had this silent pact to make sure each other got heard. After I had been given such an advantage, how could I not sit in the front row and smile for others? I think once someone has looked out for you, you never forget. I made a conscious effort to develop young people."

Sometimes Laybourne would feed these upstarts nuggets of wisdom, sometimes she'd make introductions, and sometimes she'd tell them to hit the sauce—just like her "Power Bitches." Laybourne and a bunch of women in her industry would get together to celebrate every time one of them was promoted, and these gals had a taste for tipple. "The guys would be so nervous. They'd say, 'What do you do when you all get together?' And we'd say, 'We're drinking!'" she laughs. "Now I say to women's groups, 'Don't have some serious agenda to right the wrongs of oppression. Have no agenda. Just go out drinking!' I think the biggest problem women have is this earnest desire to cross every *t* and dot every *i*. We want to be so good and buttoned up when we're really great at relationships. People like to do business with people they like. We often forget that lesson, but the truth is relationships matter."

Over sixteen years, with elbow grease and a few cocktails, Laybourne grew Nickelodeon's five-man huddle into an $8 billion monolith. As her reputation spread, people sought her out, but Laybourne couldn't meet with everyone and still do her job. So her assistant started scheduling walks with "mentees" around Central Park at 7 AM. Sometimes she'd stroll the loop and end with a cup of coffee, and other times she'd amble in the Bramble. During the years she lived on Central Park West at 64th Street, Laybourne walked with more than 100 aspirants.

"I started figuring out how I could help them," she says. "If I walk with somebody in the park, mostly I try to figure out what they're good at and what their dream is. I go through my mental Rolodex of who I can connect them with who can really help. Usually you can think of a different angle for someone, or something they should read, or another person who could help.

"That's the kind of mentoring I'm interested in," Laybourne continues. "It's about the energy of networks. I don't believe women need lifelong mentoring, like a crutch. They need a jolt every so often, a spark where someone believes in them, energizes them to better themselves or think differently. With really bright people, you just do one thing and they take off. It comes from the way I was raised, believing that women need a little extra connection. We're only on this planet to bring on the next generation. I support tons of young men as well, but I feel this extra obligation to help women."

Laybourne knew her Central Park strolls were bearing fruit, and she was sick of hearing that women didn't help each other. She decided walking was the answer. She'd founded Oxygen Media by then, so Laybourne thought her firm should sponsor a large-scale event. The company's first "Mentor's Walk" occurred in 2005 in Central Park and assembled 400 women, including stars like Meryl Streep, Marlo Thomas, and Diane von Furstenberg. Laybourne's staff carefully paired promising female professionals with luminaries in their fields, and these women hit the road to see what they could do for each other.

Oxygen then launched Mentor's Walks in ten cities around the nation, including Chicago; Washington, D.C.; Los Angeles; Denver; Colorado Springs; and Portland, Oregon. Six months before the walk, the company's representatives would meet with each city's leading women, who would then contact their networks for support. "We would arrive and end up introducing many women in the same city who had never connected to each other. They were always thrilled because we found people who would be interesting and helpful to them," Laybourne says. "My dream was that by publicizing this, we'd get women out there connecting and responding. Our mission was to change the view. If you just get women walking, talking, and sharing their thoughts, they end up doing amazing things. They open doors for each other."

Oxygen's events inspired Vital Voices, an NGO that "identifies, trains, and empowers" women leaders, to launch Women's Mentoring Walks in other countries, including Uganda, where Laybourne walked with a high school student whose dream was to attend medical school at Johns Hopkins University. Laybourne advised her to spend a year at boarding school in America to get acclimated. With permission from the girl's mother, Laybourne arranged for transcripts, recommendations, and scholarship applications, and eventually secured a spot at her husband's alma mater in Canada.

"Because of technology, this was the easiest thing and I was thrilled to do it," she says. "If I'd had to do it the old-fashioned way, making phone calls and sending FedExes, I don't know if I would have raised my hand. But because it was easy, there was no way that kid wasn't coming here."

Still, it wasn't a walk in the park, so to speak. In the end there were difficulties procuring a student visa, and on quite a few occasions Laybourne found herself on the phone with Uganda at 2 AM. But, she says, when the girl finally arrived a month late for school, it was clear why Laybourne had done it. "Men are set on a track: kill the deer, go for the goal. But women have different brains, brains structured toward a web of inclusion. We make all these connections naturally," she says. "Now technology is supporting us. I get an e-mail a week from an African or Argentine woman. It's all these women together. It's not just a U.S. thing. It's going around the globe."

Ambling Along

Gerry Laybourne isn't the only gal inspired by a good mosey. Her friend Maggie Wilderotter is also hot to trot.

In 1996, Laybourne left Nickelodeon to serve as president of Disney/ABC cable networks, and for two years she was miserable. "It just wasn't for me," she says. "It was an executive job and I was used to being an entrepreneur and a builder." She confided in Wilderotter, the only other woman on the board of the National Cable & Telecommunications Association, and Wilderotter dragged her to lunch.

"I had been pretty darn honest with her before, but we weren't seated for very long and Maggie could tell just by reading my body language. She said, 'You know what? I can't watch this. This is not for you. You gotta get out of there and I'm going to help you move on,'" Laybourne recalls. "With Maggie, it was tough love. She really walked me to the woodshed, but it was a very sisterly thing to do. She said, 'You're going to be great as a real entrepreneur.'"

Wilderotter was right. Within a year, Laybourne had partnered with Oprah Winfrey and Carsey-Werner Productions, the creator of hits like *The Cosby Show* and *Roseanne*, and she began buying up online services for women. She launched the Oxygen Network in 2000 with 10 million subscribers.

Like Laybourne, Wilderotter loves walking, especially when it's paired with solving problems and helping women. In 2008, at the Fortune "Most Powerful Women" summit in California, Wilderotter—who was by then chairman and CEO of Frontier Communications—got to know Joan Amble, who was then executive vice president and corporate comptroller of American Express. The ladies learned they were neighbors in Darien, Connecticut, so they started striding together.

On one circuit, they talked about Fortune's joint initiative with the U.S. State Department to pair accomplished American women with talented female mentees from other countries. Surely this was admirable, but what about the sponsorship gap in the United States? How could they help young women here? Recalling the joy they'd shared with prominent gals at the Fortune conference, they wondered if it was possible to stoke the friendships begun in California and work on filling the mentorship void simultaneously.

"We decided success would be (1) if we had fun, because if it's not fun there are a lot of other things we could be doing; (2) if we got together every quarter and brought a friend, because we're always looking to expand our networks; and (3) if we were able to take this impressive group of women and all we'd learned on our journey and apply that to helping other women in the U.S.," Amble says.

Amble went straight to her CEO, Ken Chenault, to discuss her plans with these new pals. He agreed that to get a return on events like Fortune's, particularly in the midst of a recession, Amble had to continue to fuel her network. Chenault offered to host, and he joined the ladies at a cocktail party preceding their reunion dinner.

Despite hectic schedules, every woman came. "We're talking about CEOs of Fortune 500 companies, women who lead M&A at major institutions, partners at law firms, consultants, women in very high positions," Amble says. "They all took the time to get together because it was meaningful to them."

At the end of dinner, Amble and Wilderotter broached their idea for a "pay-it-forward program." "Everyone agreed it was a no-brainer," says Amble, who is now president of JCA Consulting. "It was such a rich discussion." After some debate, they decided to target women four to seven years into their careers, enough time to have proven themselves in meaningful ways, but after they'd left "the protective bubble of college, a point when women can get stuck because they don't have as many people to go to." By then, mentors could assess young women's performance and identify high-potential candidates. They could spot ladies with the capacity to be both magnates and magnets for others.

To ensure their program was current and germane to the needs of a younger generation, the elders formed a focus group. They discerned that mentees desired MEN: mentoring, education, and networking. Well, *that* was inconvenient. To beef up their acronym, they added a couple of letters, settling on W.O.M.E.N. (Women Optimizing Mentoring, Education, and Networking) In America.

The younger set welcomed a rigorous application and interview process, as they wanted to feel chosen, and they prized the safety and freedom to ask "stupid" questions when necessary. "Why would

I tell my employer where I need help?" one asked. Millennials didn't want one-on-one mentoring, but rather to see an array of experiences, as if their elders' paths formed a "Choose Your Own Adventure" book that might inform their own.

Senior executives split mentees into clusters based on areas of expertise regardless of industry, including STEM (science, technology, engineering, and math), professional and corporate services (e.g., law, consulting, HR, finance), and marketing/entrepreneurship. Each cluster has about ten mentees and three or four leaders, whom Wilderotter and Amble extracted from their Fortune group and by rallying their Stiletto Networks. These are women like Ursula Burns, the chairman and CEO of Xerox, where Wilderotter is on the board; Denise Morrison, the president and CEO of Campbell Soup, who also happens to be Wilderotter's sister; Carol Hochman, the president of RHH Capital and Consulting, who was for a decade president and CEO of Triumph Apparel Corp. (formerly Danskin, Inc.); and Martha McGarry, a corporate securities partner at Skadden, Arps, who sits on the firm's governing body.

Clusters meet every six weeks, and all participants assemble three times per year to hear speakers, attend panel discussions, and participate in skill-building sessions. Mentees direct their own learning, and senior executives respond to questions and requests. When young women want to understand financial statements or learn to write business plans and get VC funding, the elders enlist experts to teach modules. When mentees want to switch fields, mentors help set up interviews.

Still, Amble says the program isn't completely Montessori. Once mentors understand their clusters' strengths, weaknesses, and leadership styles, they introduce topics they believe will be beneficial. "You can set the model," Amble says, "but it has to be personalized."

"Giving back" doesn't necessarily mean joining formal mentoring organizations, but rather making a day-to-day commitment to facilitating women's success.

W.O.M.E.N. In America compresses banker Cristina Morgan's "learn, earn, return" blueprint ("twenty years to learn, twenty years to earn, twenty years to return"), asking mentees to give back during their third and final year of the program. "Giving back" doesn't necessarily mean joining formal mentoring organizations, but rather making a day-to-day commitment to facilitating women's success. Even on the busiest weeks, why not help friends find the right jobs and opportunities? Why not have lunch with a new mother to encourage her to stay in the workforce? Why not take thirty minutes to open doors and make introductions for another woman? As Susan Lyne of Gilt Groupe pointed out, all those half-hours add up.

"Part of this is about maturing, thinking about what's important," Amble says. "Losing these women needlessly from the workforce would be a tragic thing. We try to let them know it's not going to be easy, but they have choices and they have a voice. We want to support them and give them courage. We want these women to have more confidence in themselves and the decisions they make. Having that validation is critical. We hope they'll stay in the alumnae organization, and that this will be their golf game going forward."

Mentors convene quarterly for dinner, throw a holiday party, and plan an annual "Girls' Weekend" concurrent with the Fortune summit. Spending so much time together allows each woman to place her own style and corporate culture in context. "We all approach things so differently because the cultures of our companies are so different," Amble says, remembering a time when she described something in a "very AmEx way," and another woman retorted,

"This is what you really meant!" "The way she said it was more direct, but I was hearing the way they do things at her firm. That's the excitement, that we can all be ourselves and still respect the way others operate. There is true diversity and inclusiveness here."

The elders have formed a support group as well. "So many of the young women ask how we did it with children, and we all talk about these things. They've seen us go through challenges too, and they've observed our friendships—how we help each other, how everyone has different opinions and styles, but still respects each other. It's something they want for themselves too," Amble expands. "Connecting is a very visible part of what we do, and it reinforces the importance of physical contact, not just technology. It's a natural consequence of doing something out of passion and love, allowing your friendships to be the glue."

One friendship Amble solidified through W.O.M.E.N. In America paved her way to a corporate board seat, and she now sits on three boards: Sirius XM satellite radio, Booz Allen Hamilton, and Brown-Forman, a producer of wine and spirits, where Amble is the first female independent director. "When she heard I was retiring from American Express, my friend introduced me to her partner at Heidrick & Struggles, who within weeks presented this fabulous opportunity to me. She found the perfect board. It's such a great fit, and it wouldn't have come about otherwise."

Maggie Wilderotter emphasizes that mentors are now doing business together too—and not just any deals, either. Big ones. At the Fortune summit, Wilderotter met Jennifer Nason, the global head of technology, media, and telecom investment banking at JPMorgan Chase, and she convinced Nason to join W.O.M.E.N. In America. Nason then found herself hobnobbing with an even broader group of top-flight women and, as she groomed younger gals for success, her peers witnessed her integrity and skills. Within a year, Wilderotter enlisted JPMorgan to lead Frontier Communications' $3.2 billion high-yield bond offering, the largest of its kind in 2010. She trusted Nason to steer the relationship toward the best possible results for Frontier.

"Value is created when you trust people, when you understand their capabilities and work side-by-side on projects, even if they don't have anything to do with your specific business," says Wilderotter, who is also chair of President Obama's National Security Telecommunications Advisory Committee. "Value is created through relationships, and as we have more women in the C-suite, there's more affiliation and more reasons for women to get together. We do business together and help each other, and it's been so gratifying because of the richness of the interaction. It's delightful!"

WalkStyles

In Southern California, Marilyn Alexander, a corporate director with her own consulting firm, has also formed Stiletto Networks by walking. In 2003, Alexander had recently resigned as senior vice president and CFO of the Disneyland Resort, where she oversaw two theme parks and three hotels in Anaheim. Before that, she'd worked in Orlando, Florida, a small town where she felt boxed in. "I had no network other than at Disney World. I didn't get out and see people unless it was for advertising," she says. "I went on vacation with a group of senior executives at Disney every year, but frankly, you don't relax. You still know you work for people."

Alexander spent countless hours at her job and devoted limited free time to her marriage. "I made a conscious decision not to have a separate life," she says. And it wasn't so hard, after all; as a military brat whose family moved every year, Alexander never learned to develop close ties. "I don't have a hometown and I didn't really have friends. When I left a base, I never expected to see those people again."

At age 18, Alexander started working her way through college, and by her own account she never stopped working. "I worked all the time, but I wasn't lonely," she says. "I had very few friends and rarely tried to make new friends."

When she left Disney at age 52, two years after she'd planned to retire, Alexander gave herself a three-month sabbatical, avoided recruiters' persistent calls, and decided to see if she could build a consulting practice. But as the primary breadwinner in her family, it was complicated. "I wanted desperately to retire and I would have gone to much greater lengths, but I make a multiple of what my husband makes. We made that decision a long time ago because I'm so career-oriented," she says. "So I thought if this doesn't work, I can always go take a job."

Soon after, Alexander met Sue Parks, who had just founded WalkStyles, a company devoted to helping people live active, healthy lifestyles. Parks was also a dedicated career gal who had been executive vice president of operations at Kinko's and senior vice president at Gateway. She invited Alexander to be an administrator for one of WalkStyles' cohorts, an initial group of fifty women from Orange County.

Because Alexander was consulting and had more flexibility, she became "Walk Mom" to an assembly of all sorts, from senior executives to academics to stay-at-home moms. "It was like a living focus group, a beta test for Sue's business. It's a big group, so we amoeba around, like a floating cocktail party," Alexander says. "One day a woman said, 'Marilyn, how many children do you have?' I don't have any, but they all assumed I did because I took care of everyone."

Each member set her individual goal without peer pressure, and once they'd made a commitment to walk a certain number of steps, the women stayed together. Alexander now leads a diverse crowd on Wednesdays and a more corporate set on Saturdays, and she's found walking to be a convenient, low-impact way to feel out new people. "If someone will walk with me, I'm happy to mentor her," she says. "It's hard to prioritize and do everything, but I know I'm going to take a walk anyway."

Just as with any large group, smaller cliques have solidified as members unite over common interests. "We've all met new friends and business associates. You're not supposed to solicit business, but if work is an important part of your life, you talk about it," Alexander says, highlighting that WalkStyles friends have directed clients her way and led to her second corporate board seat.

On one stroll, a woman approached and said she'd like to get to know Alexander. Because this gal was a relationship manager for a bank, work seemed an easy entrée into discourse, and Alexander soon revealed that she'd been on a corporate board. Her new friend asked if she'd be interested in joining another, and before long, Alexander was interviewing with the executive team.

What is it about walking that allows women to brainstorm and connect? "Your head is free, you're more creative. It also shows businesspeople that you don't have to show up in a suit and have a formal lunch or dinner," Alexander says. Of course, exercise robs women of the traditional clothes/shoes icebreakers, but it's also a great equalizer. The ladies can't take themselves too seriously in shorts and a jog bra, even a ritzy one made by Casall. "A bunch of us from the walk group were at a conference and didn't even recognize each other," she laughs. "We had never seen each other in regular clothes!"

Alexander didn't consider herself a joiner, and she didn't start out with close female friends. But now, if she needs anything or if she has something to share, she thinks first of her walk group and another women's group she's entered. "Both of them are networks of trust. I feel that any of the members would do the same for me as I would do for them. If I called anyone and asked for help—if I said, 'Would you walk with me to talk through this issue?'—I know she would say yes," Alexander says. "We're always giving each other free business advice. If I needed a financial planner or help with a family trust, I could call one of the women in this group. If someone comes to me for business, I will do my best to do a good job, and if I'm not the right person, I will tell them the truth. They're filled with very upstanding people.

"It's really transformed our lives," she continues. "Through these groups, I started understanding what networking between women is. It's not going to lunch and talking about business. When women get together and walk for an hour and a half, it just flows. It's business, kids, what we did this weekend. It's everything. It's true friendship."

CHAPTER 9

BIG MOTOR GIRLS

ost women aren't chief executives or even one level below. Most women didn't go to Harvard. Most women don't work at Goldman or Google. Most women weren't steeped in Silicon Valley. Most women can't hire the village. Most women are doing their best. Most women are exhausted.

"Who cares if some elite crowd is assembling behind closed doors?" they say. "What's in it for me?"

Most women should know: These aren't just prominent mainstays consolidating their power, or exceptional upstarts rattling the cage. This is happening everywhere. Women launching small businesses. Women frustrated in or laid off from corporate jobs. Women who want to reenter the workforce after having left to raise children. They're all forming and relying on Stiletto Networks.

Women want to connect. They just need to know where to start, and thousands have found an answer in Carole Hyatt. It's why Hyatt began convening women thirty years ago, and why they still gather at her home today.

Getting to Next

On a cool, crisp evening in October 2011, a night that belies the Indian summer that will engulf Manhattan the following week, the ladies are coming. One by one, women in suits and light jackets march upstairs from the B or C train or hop off the M79 bus outside the Museum of Natural History, sidestepping throngs of children who've been cooing over dinosaurs.

Evolutionary biology is not on the agenda, not for these gals. Tonight, their goal is reinvention. So they turn their backs on fossilized bones and enter the marble lobby of a white-glove apartment building across the street. They follow the doorman to a wood-paneled elevator, up to Hyatt's sixth-floor apartment.

Hyatt's foyer is mirrored floor to ceiling, and after crossing the threshold, the women see themselves from so many angles. They scribble name tags and grab light snacks, filling plates with nuts and pretzels and hummus, cups with Pellegrino and juice. On so many slick surfaces rests Hyatt's whimsical art: collages with materials scavenged at tag sales near her home in the Berkshires; Barbies in Barbie cars, fused beneath silver paint; troll dolls from the 1980s, their red and blue hair suspended in an upward blast. In Hyatt's incarnation as artist, she reverts to the past, meditating on the commercial trappings of youth. But in her role as leadership coach, she revs her engine toward the future.

Hyatt often conducts seminars in her sky-blue dining room, where two large utilitarian tables accommodate her usual fifty guests. It's a smaller crowd tonight, so participants—including the owner of a printing business and a partner in a small accounting firm who also opened a Latin dance studio—are invited to gather on acid-green couches in her acid-green living room. Hyatt flicks one switch on the wall, illuminating a green light installation beside the doorway, then stoops to reach another, lighting a neon pink table at the center of the room. Guests place cups on a Lucite rectangle filled inside with crushed beer cans. A cat named Eleanor Roosevelt skulks around the room.

Hyatt looks younger than her seventy-some years. Tonight she is dressed head-to-toe in magenta—suit, silk shirt, matching lipstick—and she perches herself on an acid-green chair at the center of an intimate semicircle. She runs fingers through her cropped golden hair and begins to speak slowly, methodically, and with warmth. The sun sinks low, casting the Hayden Planetarium as a giant, glinting disco ball outside. The "Salon for Networking" has begun.

> *Hyatt spent years analyzing women, and the more she learned, the more she realized that even the most successful ladies still needed help navigating their careers or, as Hyatt puts it, "getting to next."*

Carole Hyatt's home is mission control for her Leadership Forum, which began eighteen years ago after she sold her ground-breaking market research firm, which specialized in women and children. Hyatt spent years analyzing women, and the more she learned, the more she realized that even the most successful ladies still needed help navigating their careers or, as Hyatt puts it, "getting to next."

And Hyatt knew from experience how hard it was, coming up through the ranks. Back in the early 1960s, she'd been an entrepreneur in Manhattan and an original "Runaway Bride." Hyatt dated only to find the next person to bring home to her hopeful parents, but she had no real interest in getting married. She kept getting engaged ("four or five times"!) but always pulled the ripcord at the last second. "To my parents this was a disaster," she sighs. "They were so upset."

But she'd seen her mother stifled in marriage, a 1940s housewife "on a golden chain." Befitting her era, Hyatt's mother's role was to tend the household while her husband supported their family financially. After expanding his parents' dairy business, Hyatt's father moved his wife and children from Queens to Great Neck, Long Island, where her mother dutifully shepherded children to school and activities. Working outside the home would have been an insult to her husband, implying that he wasn't an adequate provider. Yet Hyatt knew her mother longed for more.

Hyatt's mother had a passion for real estate and would regularly visit Manhattan to scout properties. With no business background or money of her own save an allowance she received from her husband, she obviously couldn't make a grand purchase without his support. "She had talent. She just had a sense for it, a smell for what was going to happen," Hyatt recalls. "She would show my father and he would say, 'That's interesting.' But every time it came time to put up the money, he would back out. It was such a disappointment to her. Watching her was very sad to me."

While Hyatt's mother wanted her to have a husband and children, she understood when her daughter ran from marriage to pursue her first love: business. "I was so grateful to my mother because she gave me enormous permission," Hyatt says. "She said you should get married and have children *and* you should work. Having these two signals was very unusual in those days."

Hyatt had begun making her own money at age 16, doing improv with a theater group for $5 an hour. Soon, she was hooked. As her friends wed and had babies, Hyatt went to school and worked and taught. She got her master's degree and became a children's theater director, cofounding the Peppermint Players, which at its height in the early 1960s performed in four off-Broadway theaters. Eventually, Hyatt bought out her partner and sold the company's work to McGraw-Hill, which distributed Peppermint Players shows on film worldwide for fifteen years. Peter Pan Records also sold more than 1 million copies of the Players repertoire.

By 1961, Hyatt was producing children's specials as a consultant to CBS while also teaching improv at Hunter College and The New School. One night, she went on a blind date with a guy named Tully Plesser who worked in market research for an advertising agency. Plesser spent his days conducting focus groups and was intrigued when Hyatt talked about her classes. Could she use improv to solicit reactions to his clients' products and services?

Hyatt had no lesson plan for her New School class the following week, so she invited Plesser to bring food, books, and TV shows to gauge students' response. "Class," she said, "tonight we're going to make up commercials." The experiment was such a hit that by evening's end, "Tully went nuts. He said, 'Can you do this with anyone?'"

Hyatt agreed to visit Plesser's office to show his colleagues how improv worked. Curious to see if Hyatt could tap a new market, Plesser assembled a group of children. He and his peers then stood agape behind a two-way mirror, watching as Hyatt got down on the floor and played. She asked boys and girls to interact with available toys, and soon they were engaging in scenarios, talking about what they liked and disliked about each doll or truck. Hyatt was a whiz at teasing the truth out of kids.

Unbeknownst to her, Plesser had also lined up a reporter and photographer from *Sponsor* magazine to chronicle this new form of market research. A month later, the article appeared, and Hyatt's life changed forever. She got a call from a representative at Bosco, the maker of a popular children's chocolate drink. He wanted her to do a study for the company, but Hyatt demurred, insisting she didn't know anything about market research. "I just like playing with kids," she told him. "Call the agency." But the executive persisted, saying he'd like to take her to lunch and would even offer a consultant's fee for her time. Hyatt gave him forty-five minutes in the CBS cafeteria.

"I think play-acting is what children do, and this will be the answer. You're the one," he said. "I'll get you the child psychologist and the children and the two-way mirror." And he named a sum that was, for Hyatt, spectacular; Bosco would pay her $500 per session, more than she was making per week at CBS.

For the next four years, the phone would ring and Hyatt would find herself talking to someone who had read the *Sponsor* write-up. As if by accident, she had become a coveted force in the budding field of market research. Yet Hyatt knew that to maintain this rewarding side-venture while working at CBS, she'd need to partner with a child psychologist.

Hyatt was in her late twenties by then, and all her friends were paired off, at home with kids. She didn't know any women like herself—until she met June Esserman. Esserman was a child psychologist working with Dan Yankelovich, a Harvard man quickly making a name for himself in market and social behavior research. Hyatt realized that with her background in improv and Esserman's expertise in psychology, they could team up.

She was also keen to branch out as her limitations at CBS became increasingly clear. CBS managers refused to give Hyatt a producer's title, even though she was doing producer's work. "They made me an associate producer and made some guy I'd never met, who never touched these shows, the producer," Hyatt remembers. "When I asked why, they said, 'Well, you have to lift things.' And I said, 'Don't you have unions for that?' And finally, they said, 'If we make you the producer, then these other women will want to be producers too. We just don't do that.' It was the end of my TV career because I wouldn't be an associate producer."

Yankelovich invited her to join forces, and in exchange for office space and the prestige of his brand, Hyatt and Esserman launched a new child research division of his business. Hyatt brought clients like food companies, television shows, books, and the Encyclopaedia Britannica, all of which had come from the *Sponsor* magazine article. "We were using Dan's name for starters so doors would open," Hyatt says. "It had never been done before. We got very big, very fast."

But after about eight years watching Yankelovich's business explode, Hyatt and Esserman wanted to go it alone rather than give him 40 percent of their revenues. Quickly, they began to see problems. "I couldn't get a credit card; I had to get my kid brother to sign for me. No one would rent us office space; I had to bring my kid brother to sign the papers," Hyatt remembers. "I didn't know any other women running companies, but I was so hungry for this."

Yet there *were* other women like Hyatt, and they had begun to find each other. In the early 1960s, a female entrepreneur named Sandra Brown flew from Chicago to New York in search of similar women—women with "big motors," women who owned and ran their own businesses. Somehow, Brown found five women entrepreneurs, including Hyatt, and brought them all together. "I had never been so relieved in my life. None of us could get a loan from a bank, or office space, or a credit card," Hyatt says. "We'd never known about each other, but we weren't alone."

Shortly after, another woman reached out to Hyatt. She was filming a documentary on women who owned their own firms, and she had found four more. That meant there were nine!

A few years later, when Hyatt was in her late thirties, she was invited to join the New York Women's Forum, which was founded in the 1970s to convene pioneering women across a variety of fields. "By that time I had married the guy in the office next to mine at CBS and we had a daughter. I wasn't baking cookies. I was working and traveling and I felt guilty," Hyatt says. "Finally I had people to talk to, about work and about bringing up children."

The Women's Selling Game

Hyatt Esserman Research Associates was one of the first market and social behavior research companies in America to focus on children, if not the first. Soon the firm had thirty-five employees, almost all of them female, and the bosses created a "lifestyle-friendly" environment before such a term existed. After school and during vacations, they would set up two rooms with toys for their children. As kids got older, they put them to work, paying them to tally questionnaire results. Clients never questioned the presence of children in the office.

In the late 1960s, Hyatt and Esserman noticed changes happening in the workforce. Suddenly, women weren't available to do focus groups during office hours because they were working or going back to school. Hyatt started to get calls from women saying, "I'm a friend of so-and-so and I need ten minutes of your time. I would like to get a job, or I'm thinking about starting my own business."

There wasn't time to meet with all of them individually, so Hyatt hosted tutorials in her conference room on the last Friday of every month. Before long, fifty women were attending each session and Hyatt was renting a hotel ballroom. Ladies kept asking the same question: Where can I find an agent or salesperson? They had great ideas for businesses, but they all wanted someone else to sell for them. "I said, 'You're the one who has to sell!'" Hyatt exclaims. "It was so obvious they would never have anything big if they couldn't sell for themselves, but they felt it was dirty, ultimately like being a prostitute."

Hyatt began teaching women to sell. She'd put a tiny ad in the *New York Times* and 250 ladies would appear, and soon she was conducting workshops called "The Women's Selling Game" all over the city. To educate students about different industries, Hyatt often invited notable businesspeople to her classes. One evening, she welcomed the owner of a series of custom shirt shops, expecting him to deliver a brief speech about scale and franchising. Instead, he arrived with a nude mannequin and spent much of class stroking its breasts as he lectured female students on the ins and outs of his trade. When he left, the ladies were up in arms. Why would Hyatt expose them to this outrageous boor?

> *These women needed to toughen up. Their ventures would never flourish if they stayed coddled in a classroom, preaching to the converted.*

Hyatt understood their point, but she also knew the mishap provided a valuable lesson. These women needed to toughen up. They had to realize it wasn't going to be easy. Their ventures would never flourish if they stayed coddled in a classroom, preaching to the converted. The real world of business wasn't some cul-de-sac of female patronage, and they should expect to meet all sorts of unsavory characters. The real question was: How were they going to deal with it? Could they laugh in the face of sexism, press forward, and prove themselves against the odds?

Hyatt's first book, also called *The Women's Selling Game*, became a nationwide bestseller, and around 1973, Hyatt and Esserman embarked on a second market research business focused on this new breed of working women. From all her studies and seminars, Hyatt realized the skills she was teaching were important, but what women wanted most was a network. If they couldn't assimilate with men, they were determined to create their own. They'd find peers who cared and took them seriously. "They wanted to know each other," Hyatt says. "They'd ask questions and I'd answer, and then they formed a support group. They really started to help each other."

The Pacer

Carole Hyatt and June Esserman's partnership was a model for other women. Networking and helping each other was exactly what they did—until they didn't. For the first five years of their eighteen-year collaboration, the two women worked seamlessly. Hyatt brought in clients and created new methodologies to study responses, while Esserman served as the in-house analytical engine. But after half a decade working side-by-side, they'd learned each other's areas of expertise and their competition began.

Hyatt wrote a book, so Esserman wrote a book. Hyatt wrote another. Hyatt brought in a client, so Esserman brought in two. Esserman added a staff member, so Hyatt added two. They questioned each other's judgment in front of underlings. "I would subvert her staff. I'd say, 'Have you ever considered doing this? Why did June think this was a good idea?'" Hyatt admits. "She would do

the same with my staff: 'What's happening with so-and-so client?'
It was like a marriage, where all these little things happen."

Esserman's procrastination made Hyatt crazy. Esserman worked
like a college kid, staying up late before a big presentation and forcing
the company's typing pool to pull all-nighters along with her.
Sometimes she would still be writing on the flight to a meeting,
and when she arrived she'd approach the client's typing pool to
prepare her work. Hyatt hated this slapdash approach. "It drove
me and our clients nuts. I wouldn't even know what I was present-
ing until the page arrived!" Hyatt says. "I tried everything, even
lying about the date of the presentation, but she would call the
client and figure it out."

Hyatt never liked competition. It made her angry and jealous
that Esserman could be her partner, yet also her rival. So it wasn't
until 1982—after Esserman, who was only 55, had a heart attack in
their Madison Avenue office and died—that Hyatt realized the true
worth of their battle. "We loved each other, but we were also highly
competitive. It was hard for our staff, but very good for our
business. It was the reason we were so successful," Hyatt says. "June
was my pacer, the person who pushed me to think, to be smarter
and compete. She really made my motor go. But I didn't know that
until I wrote her eulogy."

Today, Hyatt believes she would handle things differently.
"Instead of getting angry and upset, I would say June was a genius.
She *was*. I would tell the staff and the typing pool, 'This is our most
important person and this is how she works. It gives her the motor,
the energy, and the brilliance. You may have to stay up all night
doing a report and then you'll have the next day off. If you can't
handle it, then don't come on board,'" she reflects. "Again, I didn't

realize that until she died. Anyone who is brilliant and has idiosyncratic behavior—look at Steve Jobs—is going to get scolded. But you figure out how to work around it if this is the genius, the person so good we can't live without her."

As it happens, Hyatt Esserman Research Associates could not live without her.

When Esserman died, Hyatt sold the business quickly, and then she went to bed. "I really couldn't get up," Hyatt says. "I was in deep mourning." Still, she had speaking engagements on her calendar, auditoriums full of women eager to learn the "Women's Selling Game." So occasionally, Hyatt would be at home in her pajamas and realize she had to fly to Pittsburgh. "I would go out and say, 'Yay! Yay! Yay! You can do it!'" she says. "And then I'd come back and go to bed."

One day, Hyatt's doorbell rang. It was 4 PM and there was her neighbor, Linda Gottlieb. Gottlieb had a thriving career in children's films, and the two women had bonded over their shared love of clothes. Hyatt owned a beautiful pocketbook Gottlieb would borrow for formal engagements, and a jacket Gottlieb considered her good luck charm. She'd wear it every time she was selling a film. But today Gottlieb was holding a pink slip.

"She said, 'I don't know why I'm here. I've just been fired. I'm supposed to be in the Russian Tea Room and I can't go. Everyone is talking about me, and I feel like a failure,'" Hyatt recalls. When she noticed Hyatt was still in her nightgown and robe, she asked what was wrong. Was Hyatt sick?

"I feel like I've failed," Hyatt replied. "I had to sell the company very fast. I had to let go of all my people. I feel like a failure."

Hyatt and Gottlieb both felt isolated and ashamed. Each woman's identity was inextricably tied to her work, and when they lost their jobs, they lost a part of themselves. They began to meet up every day, at first commiserating and then thinking maybe they could collaborate or help each other.

Shortly after, Hyatt attended the Women's Forum's first national conference. The primary topic of discussion was how to handle success, but, Hyatt remembers, one woman stood up and said, "'I have no problem with success. Success is easy! It's my failure that's a problem.' Every woman in that room started to stand up and talk about failure."

Here were bright, driven women at the helm of their own companies or running divisions of major firms. Many had arrived by hired car and were dressed in designer clothes they'd purchased with their own paychecks. They had every reason to celebrate their accomplishments, but still they shined a spotlight on shortcomings. Still they never felt good enough.

When Hyatt got home, she went straight to see Gottlieb. She knew what they had to pursue.

The two women began to interview superstars about their failures, including Steve Jobs, who had lost his job at Apple; Walter Cronkite, who had been pushed out of CBS; and George McGovern, who had run for president and lost. In 1987, *When Smart People Fail* became another bestseller and pulled Hyatt out of her depression. Ladies from the Women's Forum rallied around her, and again Hyatt began speaking to groups, this time about managing transitions.

Lady Bountifuls

The New York Women's Forum was one of the first places ambitious gals like Hyatt could connect with like-minded peers, women who understood their unique business and personal issues. These ladies were forging ahead despite sexism and discrimination. There weren't many of them in any one company or even within entire professions, so they looked outside their industries to female leaders in other fields.

"There were very few women. It was lonely. You kept your head down, you did what you could do, you thought you were reinventing the wheel, and if you were promoted it was because you were that good," says Davia Temin, a member of the Women's Forum who has been a featured speaker at Hyatt's Leadership Forum.

> *"In most companies, there was a certain inadvertent pitting of women against each other, because if there's only going to be one woman allowed at the top, then it's you or me."—Davia Temin*

Men could afford to be collegial. They developed strong relationships with colleagues because they knew they would rise together, but it was different for the token women. "In most companies, there was a certain inadvertent pitting of women against each other, because if there's only going to be one woman allowed at the top, then it's you or me," Temin continues. "Women had to go outside of our organizations because it was so competitive within. We had to develop horizontal networks. And then you find you've all been in similar situations. You learn stuff. You say, 'Wow, that happened to you too? How did you handle it?' and it gives you another arrow in the quiver."

Temin led corporate marketing at several large financial institutions—including, most recently, GE Capital Services, reporting directly to the president and CEO, Gary Wendt—before founding her own crisis and reputation management firm, Temin and Company. She says that when she worked at Wertheim Schroder &

Co. in the 1990s, the only female partner was relegated to an office in a distant corner on another floor. "She had made so much money so they couldn't not make her partner, but she said, 'They put me here so they don't have to see me every day.'"

When female employees wanted to talk shop with other skirts, they absconded to a Chinese restaurant on Tenth Avenue, far from the office so colleagues wouldn't catch on. "They were so skittish about how it would look if women were getting together. I thought it was stupid because I worked for the CEO, but I understood it," Temin says. "There was a heightened level of sensitivity. I was there for quite a while and I don't remember another woman ever making partner."

In this way, the nation's most powerful businesswomen began coming together decades ago. They often did so secretly, so as not to appear to their male bosses and peers to be "organizing." Many of their alliances emerged informally and without agenda, as a search for genuine connection among ladies breathing rarefied air.

Carole Hyatt was a witness to this trend, and she developed her Leadership Forum to help women with "big motors" find each other. In the early days, Hyatt catered to executives in the Women's Forum and A-list businesswomen like Nancy Evans, who cofounded iVillage, and Carolee Friedlander, owner of the eponymous jewelry business. Hyatt began hosting "Getting to Next" workshops and Networking Salons in her Manhattan apartment and at her house in the Berkshires. She knew women were always interested in seeing one another's homes, and she knew that being in a comfortable setting, as opposed to a boardroom, would help them relax. Her salons felt more like parties than meetings.

Still, Hyatt's events were strategic. They were meant to foster alliances to help women get ahead in all areas of life. "All sorts of creative things happen when you just get smart women talking," Hyatt says. The key was to get them asking, too. From her years in market research, Hyatt knew that women have a hard time requesting career help or advice. "Women could ask about anything—a hairdresser, a manicurist, a doctor—but if there was money involved, they felt terrible. You didn't want to ask a friend to get you business. If you ever asked for anything, you'd have to give back double to make it okay."

Hyatt formalized the process so that every woman in the room was forced both to ask for something she needed and offer something she could provide. The two didn't have to be related. "I made it easier. It didn't have to be a barter. It was more like: 'You get me a client, I'll get you a vacation,'" Hyatt says. "We all love being 'Lady Bountifuls' and giving. When you can give, it's not so hard to ask." One female executive who was fighting cancer offered up all her research and contacts to any woman who was also diagnosed.

As years passed and women became a greater force in large corporations, Hyatt worked with firms like Deloitte & Touche and Infiniti cars to help strengthen networks of female employees. She convened women across divisions who struggled because relating to colleagues and clients was no longer straightforward. Can a man take a female client for cocktails at night, or vice versa? Wouldn't such an invitation be misconstrued? What if women weren't interested in golf? Many ladies were too busy to break for lunch, and they focused on their families on weekends. How could they connect personally with clients, and with each other?

Attending Hyatt's Leadership Forum allowed women across business units to give tips and solicit guidance. What's the best way to get on the calendar for a presentation to the C-suites? What questions might higher-ups ask? What steps should I take to get promoted?

"By then there were so many more women in upper and middle management holding the money bags, so how do you get them to release some of it for you?" Hyatt says. "We built friendships and trust between equals who may not have otherwise met. We came up with creative strategies for how to build relationships the female way, which is different from the men's way. Men play golf or basketball together and they're pursuing a common interest, but most women think you're not building a relationship that way. Women have different needs."

Women Presidents

More than 2,500 women have participated in Leadership Forum events, and during the past decade, Hyatt's business model has shifted as companies developed initiatives to support top female talent. Many firms now work hard to retain women at the upper echelon, but ladies in the middle still struggle. Maybe they're smart and motivated, but in the wrong role. Maybe they want more flexibility. Maybe they want to switch fields. Maybe they're dissatisfied and don't know what they want, but they're trying to figure it out.

These are the women who have each paid $45 and gathered in Hyatt's apartment that October evening. They listen intently to networking tips from a featured speaker, then break into groups of two to practice their elevator pitches. In the exercise Hyatt has designed, each one must say who she is, what she does, why she's the best at it, and what she needs to get ahead. Women then offer a skill or service they can provide to anyone in the group.

These aren't self-identifying "power chicks" busting through glass ceilings, and they don't have the bling of fancy titles at marquee firms. But with so many asks and offers, they're mirroring The Vault, 4C2B, PE WIN, ChIPs, and Babes in Boyland. Each has friends and associates who might become the client of another participant, given the right introduction or recommendation.

Even in the current recession, there are millions of women just like this, women who in aggregate represent an increasingly dominant force in American business. According to the Center for Women's Business Research, 8 million U.S. businesses are majority-owned by women, and these firms have an economic impact of $3 trillion annually. They've created and maintained 23 million jobs, or 16 percent of total jobs in the United States. The number of women-owned businesses is growing twice as fast as the number of total businesses.

Marsha Firestone, the founder and president of the Women Presidents' Organization (WPO), says that women leave corporations to start their own businesses at around age 40, which is consistent with the demographic at Hyatt's Leadership Forum. "They gain confidence after being successful in the corporate environment, and they recognize they can do it better, more lucratively, on their own. They can have more control of their time. If they have children, they can fit them into their lives in a way they can't if they're corporate employees," Firestone says. "These women say, 'I have a certain level of expertise. I want a bigger piece of the pie. I want more control.' So they go off and start their own ventures."

> *"Today a lot of companies burn people out. Men have been brought up to suck it up and not question as much, but when women say, 'Here are things we need to change,' it benefits men too."— Pernille Spiers-Lopez*

WPO helps female entrepreneurs with multimillion-dollar businesses accelerate growth and enhance competitiveness. Its 1,600 members (in 100 chapters on five continents) run companies with average revenue of $13 million and aggregate revenue of $17 billion. Some of WPO's fastest-growing companies fall into environmental technology and IT—certainly not, Firestone underscores, all "cookies and crafts."

"The worry I have is that men are not taking it seriously enough, so a lot of competence is leaving the best companies," says Pernille Spiers-Lopez, who until 2011 led global human resources at Ikea, and before that was president of Ikea North America. She too sees women leaving large companies in droves to launch businesses, and she believes this trend will continue. "Today a lot of companies burn people out. Men have been brought up to suck it up and not question as much, but when women say, 'Here are things we need to change,' it benefits men too. My son will not accept the way we worked twenty years ago; he and his peers will want to be more involved fathers."

Spiers-Lopez, who is based in Chicago, recalls being struck by the vigor of female founders when she spoke at a Women's Leadership Exchange symposium a few years ago. "I went to this conference with no expectations, but when I walked into a room of 800 women entrepreneurs, I saw the power," she says. "They all wanted to be successful and weren't necessarily competing because their businesses were anything from consulting firms to restaurants." It was enough to convince her that Ikea should engage small-business owners, specifically women, as a growing segment of customers.

"If you're part of top leadership, you need to support this changing environment so that women can thrive. If I were a CEO of a large company, I'd be looking seriously at this. I'd be concerned," Spiers-Lopez continues. "These women were really seriously preparing themselves to be a stronger part of the future. This could be the engine that drives the American economy forward."

SHAKE YOUR MONEYMAKER

omentum is building and, as Gerry Laybourne said, female connectivity is contagious. It's spreading across the globe. Links are radiating outward, breaking the barriers of business to enfold nonprofit and philanthropic circles too.

"Not only am I seeing new networks, self-created and ones that came from dust, but I'm also seeing existing networks rethinking their missions. They're coming together to find synergies," says Jacki Zehner, the youngest woman and first female trader ever to be named partner at Goldman Sachs. Zehner and her husband, who was also a Goldman partner, made a bundle when the firm went public in 1999, and she retired a few years later to devote herself to philanthropy—specifically, to empowering women and girls. "There's a growing sense that this is a period in history where we are not only imagining but knowing that if we get together and push, we'll take a giant leap forward."

"It's why I barely have time to go to the bathroom," laughs Zehner, who is now CEO of Women Moving Millions (WMM), a nonprofit whose members donate $1 million or more to organizations and initiatives that advance the fairer sex. "I have never been busier. It's rooted in the funding space, and this is the tipping point."

WMM has generated $240 million for more than 100 women's organizations, and in September 2012, Zehner stood on a stage in Tribeca, bouncing her booty to Beyoncé's "Run the World (Girls)" with legendary model and entrepreneur Tyra Banks. WMM had partnered with JPMorgan to host an "Evening of Spark" for a room full of female power players. Banks, a new member of WMM, delivered the keynote after Gloria Steinem made introductions. Worlds, as they say, were colliding.

At the WMM dinner, one thing was clear: Once women realize the impact they can have on their companies, suddenly that's not enough. Why stop at a company when there's a whole planet that needs fixing? For many successful women, for-profit and nonprofit endeavors now go hand-in-hand. Ladies are activating their business networks to champion worthy causes and, simultaneously, female executives are realizing they can leverage nonprofit board positions to forge strategic alliances with leaders in other fields. Philanthropy allows women to expand their networks, which in turn benefits their firms. One hand washes the other. This ain't their mama's church bake sale.

These women have learned that equality doesn't happen when they hoard their riches; equality results when women use their newfound fiscal might to influence policy, when they shake their moneymakers on behalf of others. Equality—and with it, comprehensive social change—occurs when there's a fusion of head and heart and means, when good intentions combine with the knowledge, business training, and funds to propel projects forward.

Philanthropy allows women to expand their networks, which in turn benefits their firms. One hand washes the other. This ain't their mama's church bake sale.

Surely it wasn't always this way, as Zehner's friend Helen LaKelly Hunt confirms. Hunt, an oil heiress in her sixties and the cofounder of WMM, learned while doing doctoral research on the origin of American feminism that women didn't fund the suffrage movement. Working with feminist historians and experts in women's philanthropy, Hunt found that women had been generous throughout millennia. They'd established hospitals, libraries, and religious institutions and they'd supported education, typically donating to their husbands' alma maters. And when it came to the right to vote, American women were tenacious and iron-willed, and many went on hunger strikes. Yet Hunt discovered by reading letters from the era that women's support seldom equaled dollars. They failed to finance female advancement.

At that point in her studies, Hunt had already begun giving, and giving big. She knew other women were giving too, so she figured there had to be enough ladies who understood that to make an impact, volunteer work must be coupled with cash. Hunt and her sister, Swanee—who served as ambassador to Austria in the 1990s and is director of the Women and Public Policy Program at Harvard's Kennedy School of Government—launched WMM in 2007 as a groundbreaking initiative, proclaiming that for the first time in history, women of high net worth were flexing their financial muscle on behalf of women and girls. The sisters led the charge with initial "spark capital" of $10 million.

"I said to donors, 'Ladies, we're making history! We keep complaining that we're left out of history, so let's show up,'" Hunt says.

She recounted a trip she took with her husband to New Guinea where, not surprisingly, men stalked prey while women cared for huts and children collectively. "Men are defined by autonomy and self-reliance, but women are relational. We're wired to connect. We've known this, but never before has it reached this area of money. We have never as women pooled our financial clout."

Hunt casts WMM as a contribution to culture, maintaining that gender parity yields more secure, high-performing societies. "If you stabilize the woman, she in turn will stabilize the family, and then the community. If you can educate the woman, she will educate her family," she says. "This looks like philanthropy, but we're not just giving. This is an investment."

ToGetHerThere

WMM has begun working with the Girl Scouts, which is revamping its image in honor of its 100th anniversary. This makeover is spearheaded by Davia Temin, the crisis management and marketing expert who serves as the Girl Scouts' first vice chair and chair of fund development, the number two gal in an organization with 3.2 million volunteers and 59 million living alumnae.

As an only child raised in Cleveland, Temin sold more Girl Scout cookies than anyone in her state, and she says the Girl Scouts provided a window onto entrepreneurship that wouldn't have opened otherwise. "I didn't have entrepreneurs in my family. They were all corporate people or teachers or scientists," she says. "When I got to be successful in my own company, the only person other than me who wasn't surprised was my mom. She said, 'Well, you sold so many cookies!'"

One evening a few years ago, Temin found herself at dinner talking to other female leaders who'd also led cookie sales in their states. What was the correlation? Had the Girl Scouts armed them with tools to achieve in life, or had they been attracted to Girl Scouts because they were wired to succeed? Either way, Temin thought, there was certainly a parallel, and perhaps you could map it: cookies sold on the x-axis and some measure of lifelong accomplishment on the y-axis. There was, she saw, some Girl Scout Cookie Indicator of Success.

Temin had triumphed by anyone's standards, and for most of her life, she'd been the only woman in the boardroom. "I wasn't ever a feminist or interested in any of this when I was in college because I never felt there were limits on what I could do," she says. "But I got into the world of finance and all of a sudden it hit me in the face."

When she was in her late thirties and met "the man I love and wanted to be with forever," Temin found she no longer needed to be around as many guys. One day she turned to her husband and declared, "You know, I'm not sure I feel like only making rich white men richer anymore."

"How about making black men richer?" he smirked.

No, they concurred, it was the "men thing" she had tired of, and at the end of her days, she wanted to have made the world better for women as well. Temin developed a stake in female advancement, joining the Harvard Kennedy School's Women's Leadership Board, becoming a senior adviser to women's councils at several commercial and investment banks, and signing on as a founding board member of the White House Project, whose ultimate goal is to see a woman elected president.

When Temin joined the Girl Scouts board, she began to drive that old outfit into the future. The Girl Scouts, she says, is the original Old Girls' Network, but the organization has not historically tapped its base for fundraising. When Temin initially approached the head of development about a 100th anniversary target, she was told their goal should be $10 million, but perhaps they couldn't muster that much. Perhaps, the woman said, the Girl Scouts should reduce its aspirations.

"I listened to this, and I just thought: *Really?* 3.2 million volunteers and 59 million alumnae? Even if they each gave you only a couple bucks?" Temin sighs. "It just struck me as lame."

Temin knew progress was tied to the power of the purse, but that purse need not be Prada or Chanel. If the Girl Scouts were able to galvanize all 113 of its councils plus loyal alumnae, then money could come from the masses. Just look at what the Obama campaign pulled off during its first election.

"Girl Scouts evokes a strong, primal, emotional response in women. It's where you told ghost stories by the campfire eating marshmallows with your girlfriends. The first time you went away from your parents was to Girl Scouts camp," Temin says. "And it's where leadership journeys are unveiled for women—journeys keyed to different age groups, to help little girls discover, connect, and take action to make the world a better place."

Just as Mattel has morphed Barbie from a Dreamhouse-coveting, pink-Corvette-driving, Ken-chasing soubrette into a gung-ho career girl, the Girl Scouts has worked to refresh its brand, aiming to be more relevant and teach girls the skills they'll need in the workplace. The Girl Scouts developed programs and badges in the STEM disciplines and created a Gold Award for girls who are shaping society. One winner built a library for a school in India, while another helped create an artificial arm for a child who'd lost hers.

Temin describes the leadership campaign, "ToGetHerThere," as all-encompassing, with posters showing girls climbing mountains, flying airplanes, and visiting the Eiffel Tower. Just as women have done for millennia, these young ladies thrive in teams, linking arms and running headfirst toward the future. "It's leadership of yourself, your family, your school, your community, your states, your company. Leadership can be writ small or large," Temin says. "Eighty percent of women in Congress were Girl Scouts, and that's on both sides of the aisle."

> *Temin met weekly with the Girl Scouts board to set an audacious goal that would inspire their nonprofit to evolve. They knew that $1 billion would command attention.*

Temin beams with pride, her voice rising with emotion at the café at the Four Seasons Hotel in midtown Manhattan. She brushes back strawberry-blond hair and adjusts the high collar on her silk shantung jacket. This woman favors bold color in all things—bright red and orange and pink, in lipsticks and jewelry and clothes. It suits her, and her message is clear: Go big or go home.

For three years, Temin met weekly with the Girl Scouts board to set an audacious goal that would inspire their nonprofit to evolve. They knew that $1 billion would command attention. "We decided to say it's all in, everything counts. It'll take five to eight years, but this way we get to stretch our muscles," Temin says. "At the end of it, when someone asks, 'How much is a girl worth?' you can say it starts at $1 billion and goes up from there."

Girl Scouts board members are now recognizing the importance of contributing financially, which didn't used to be the case. "The idea that you support what you love not only with your time, energy, and love, but also with your financial resources has been an evolving thing for them," Temin says. "Some women still shy away from the ask, or the big ask. Sometimes we shut ourselves down before we even start, but the stakes are just too high. We've gotta get over ourselves on this one!"

Because Temin spent much of her life working in finance, she understands the power of cash to steer and sustain the causes she holds dear. It was, after all, in the financial world that Temin got over her own phobia of money. She worked with VC and private equity firms, invested in stocks, and facilitated IPOs, and now she applies the same analytical flair to nonprofits. "Raising money in the private sector translates not to bake sales but to raising major money in the not-for-profit arena as well—not being afraid to ask for it and be turned down, not lowering your expectations, not backing down," she says. "Also, my area of expertise is marketing strategy, branding, advertising, visibility, and reputation, and the Girl Scouts needed to have its reputation and public image refreshed. My professional skills are what they need."

Temin still worries that most women view cash only as a way to buy *things*, instead of as a route to safety, security, and political power. During the past few years, she's encouraged the Girl Scouts board to—as the Scout song says—"make new friends, but keep the old." They've roped in more prominent ladies like Temin who bring passion, business acumen, and courage born of experience. These are women who see the ills of the world and press the full weight of their time, talent, and treasure to create solutions.

"The reason I did this is because I was so sick of being the only woman in the room, either in investment banking or at G.E. I'd say, 'Why aren't there more women?' and they'd say, 'There aren't enough women in the pipeline.' I knew there were, but 'Fine,' I said. 'I'm going straight to the pipeline.' That's what I've been pushing for, to build the pipeline," Temin booms. "Let's make sure there's a today- and future-oriented network that girls want to join.

Reaching gender equity within one generation—that's our goal. We want 'to get her there.' In the boardroom. In a political caucus. At a fire station. We've been undergoing a transformation of major proportion, and this needs to be supported by financial contributions from women."

Temin doesn't just preach from a pulpit; she lives her message every day. Now, at the firm she founded in 1997, Temin coaches twenty-two CEOs, one-quarter of whom are women. Temin and Company has ten employees, eight of whom are female, and two of whom work from homes in California and Florida. She posts pictures of her chief of staff's newborn son on Facebook, and her plush offices feel like home, warm and overflowing with Asian antiques. "I don't necessarily try to [have a majority-female firm] but I suppose it's because of my vision and my sensibility," Temin says. "We have such a smooth-running place. People respect and like each other. We're having fun. Everybody works like crazy. It's a wonderful group, and it's women. Now I'm totally okay making rich white men richer because it means I can pay the women working for me!"

Increasingly, Temin finds her worlds intersecting as ladies she knows from business are also cropping up at her favorite charities. "It feels like a harmonic convergence in the world, just like you get people winning the Nobel Prize who've done the same research in many different places. We have women from different spheres coming together with the same agenda and the same goals. We run into each other over and over again," says Temin, who also "Rocked the Mall" in Washington, D.C., with 250,000 Girl Scouts at a 100th anniversary concert in June 2012. "This fall I had seven huge women's events in seven weeks. At the end I felt like somebody should give me a shot of testosterone. I asked my husband to talk to me about basketball!"

Nonprofit work is one more vehicle helping women find their tribes, and these tribes prove helpful in all areas of life. Put simply, it's no coincidence that Karen Seitz met Shauna Mei at a Girl Scouts dinner and that they bonded despite their age difference. Both align themselves with organizations that embody their values, and these groups create another filter, winnowing the crowd and attracting donors and volunteers who share ethics and interests. Ladies see each other in action and—as with Maggie Wilderotter and Jennifer Nason—they then have a basis to decide if they'd like to do business together too.

This trend is accelerating with younger generations who were inculcated in a culture of volunteerism. Gen Y and Millennials started young, if only to pad college applications and résumés, and many have incorporated social mandates into their businesses or founded 501(c)(3)s alongside their fledgling firms. A generation ago, students may have instituted recycling programs in their high schools, buying blue and green buckets to place next to standard-issue gray, taping posters to tiled walls, exhorting classmates to "Think Globally, Act Locally." But kids raised on the Internet know that forever more, they'll need to think *and* act as citizens of the world.

Founders like Alexa von Tobel are adopting the Bill Gates model, confronting world crises and distributing wealth during their lifetimes, as opposed to issuing a bequest at death. Her company, LearnVest, has an altruistic aim, to teach women financial literacy. And after von Tobel completed a college summer internship in the village of Lwala, Kenya, for 85 Broads, she also cofounded a nonprofit called Lwala to help combat HIV and AIDS in Africa. Good works earned her a place at a four-day social entrepreneurship retreat hosted by Sir Richard Branson in

2010 on Necker Island, his private Caribbean oasis, where she met even more industry leaders devoted to creating a healthier, more just civilization.

As this overlap occurs, nonprofit lessons and principles seep into business too, as Davia Temin learned in May 2012, when she sat in the front row of St. Paul's Cathedral in London, facing the Dalai Lama. Temin and three friends from Swarthmore College, her alma mater, had collaborated on the nomination that won the Buddhist leader the £1.1 million Templeton Prize, which honors a living person who has played an exceptional role in affirming life's spiritual dimension. Upon her return from London, Temin found herself crafting a speech for a CEO in which she used the word "compassion" three times.

"It just felt right, and it's totally congruent with this person too. This is a challenging time and I realize I have the opportunity to work with people at crisis points," she says. "At any point, you can take a high road or a lower road. I can actually help nudge to the higher plane, which is also really better for business. I am a writ-large capitalist, but I believe there's a way you can meld both of these things. You can do good and do well, especially in this day of shared value. You can add value to a bottom line by doing the right thing too.

"Many of us had to shoehorn our way into a completely male world," Temin continues, "so there's one level of network that provides solace and comfort. But now we're taking it to the next level, which is actually to create value in the world. Something hits you and you realize life is finite. You realize you'd better start yelling, get that bullhorn out. I'm driven now. I want to change things, better things big-time. There's a Quaker saying I saw at a bench at Swarthmore: *Let your life speak.*"

Binders of Women

Women's sway isn't confined to religious or charity work anymore, and ladies are no longer content to sweat behind the scenes. Victories in business have led to leadership in philanthropy, which—in a crescendo of power—has now progressed to assertion in politics for women like Melanie Sabelhaus.

Sabelhaus felt blessed in 1997 when she took her company public. She was suddenly very wealthy and could easily retire, but as the daughter of an Ohio steelworker, Sabelhaus had always worked. As CEO of Exclusive Interim Properties, she'd led her seventy-five employees through four mergers and an IPO, and she'd remained on the board of the combined firm, BridgeStreet Accommodations, for a year before retiring. But now she sat at home in her pink St. John knit suit, not knowing what to do or where to go next.

When her husband returned from a meeting of the United Way Tocqueville Society, whose members give at least $10,000 annually, they started talking. Why weren't there more women on this list of donors? Sabelhaus's husband, the Tocqueville Society chair for Central Maryland, had just learned of a lady in North Carolina, Bonnie McElveen-Hunter, who was pursuing women to donate at high levels. He thought Sabelhaus should take up the mantle in their home city of Baltimore. "Most people would never think of asking a woman for $10,000," Sabelhaus says. "But I believed the reason women hadn't given was because they hadn't been asked."

Sabelhaus began reaching out to women of "influence and afflu-ence," founding the Baltimore United Way Women's Leadership Initiative. In 2001, she rallied forty-six women to donate $10,000 each, and before long she was working with McElveen-Hunter—the founder and CEO of Pace Communications, a leading custom publishing company—to take the campaign national. More than a decade later, their initiative has raised close to $1 billion.

In 2004, when McElveen-Hunter became the first woman in history to chair the American Red Cross, she brought Sabelhaus along. Sabelhaus joined the Red Cross board in 2005 and became vice chair of philanthropy in 2011, and the women conspired to change the Red Cross's approach to fundraising. McElveen-Hunter and Sabelhaus believed the Red Cross should be prepared to mobilize immediately when crises occur instead of pursuing reactive, episodic solicitations in the wake of natural disasters. Of course, this meant board members would need to step up.

"Board members thought they came with time and talent, but we said we're a fundraising board too," Sabelhaus says. "It's been peer-to-peer. We're saying 'Will you join me?'" Even in a recession, the organization found their case compelling. The National Board of Governors more than tripled donations. Nearly 90 percent of local board members now participate, and they gave close to $9 million in 2012 alone.

In 2006, McElveen-Hunter and Sabelhaus also launched the Tiffany Circle, a philanthropic effort within the Red Cross that was named to honor Northern and Southern women who united after the Civil War. Each group contributed $5,000 to commission the Tiffany stained-glass windows that now grace the Red Cross's headquarters. Thus far, Tiffany Circles have raised $44 million from more than 1,000 women, 280 of whom contribute at the $100,000 level. "We wanted to walk in these incredible women's footsteps," Sabelhaus says. "No one thought it would work, but we've gone all over the U.S. and brought hundreds of women along. Our women's initiative was the most successful pilot in the history of the Red Cross. No one could believe it."

> *Sabelhaus urges women to put their names on grants, saying they must "give out loud" to inspire other ladies of means to do the same. It may not be in women's nature to brag, but in these situations, "Anonymous" is for sissies.*

Sabelhaus now spreads her message internationally too, reaching out to women in countries like the U.K. and Japan, which lack a robust culture of philanthropy. "This is a global movement, and women are now asking other women. We now have seventeen chapters of Tiffany Circles around the world. These women come to our summit every year because they want to go back and replicate our model in their own countries," Sabelhaus continues. "We introduce it by going straight to their powerful businesswomen because other women will respect their lead. We get together at someone's home because women like to go to each other's houses and look at each other's stuff. And we talk about our kids, our businesses, our lives, all of our passions. Then we get down to the business of philanthropy."

Sabelhaus urges women to put their names on grants, saying they must "give out loud" to inspire other ladies of means to do the same. It may not be in women's nature to brag, but in these situations, "Anonymous" is for sissies. And the pressure Sabelhaus puts on other women is working. In 2009, she rose to the stage at a Red Cross event and offered participants the "opportunity" to become a "Bonnie McElveen-Hunter Tiffany Circle Lifetime Member" by contributing $100,000. "Will you join me?" she asked. Sixty-one women and one man stood up.

"You should have heard the chairs squeaking on that marble floor! In less than a minute, we raised $6.1 million from women. We will never forget that moment," she exclaims. "Not one of them picked up the phone to call her husband. We don't ask permission anymore."

Each time one of Sabelhaus's nonprofits needs help, she calls her Power Chicks or Chicks in Charge, a Stiletto Network whose members are also active in business, community, and philanthropic ventures. She asks them to chair a committee, purchase a table, persuade friends to buy tickets, and tap younger women to help further the work. "It's our golf course—these strong, vibrant, powerful circles. And we've hit the big time, with $10,000, $100,000, $1 million gifts," she says. "This is probably why I'm here on earth."

Sabelhaus, who was deputy administrator of the U.S. Small Business Administration (appointed by President George W. Bush), operates in political circles too, working to shape policy and enact social change. She served for three years as a political adviser for Women Impacting Public Policy (WIPP), a bipartisan effort to raise funds and visibility for women's issues, and at the request of Elizabeth Dole, she chaired the Women's Majority Network, an effort by prominent Republican Party women to gain access to and authority over politicians. For $25,000 minimum, women dined at exclusive lunches with GOP leaders like Mitt Romney and John McCain. Rather than comb through "binders of women" for qualified female leaders (as Romney claimed he'd done while governor of Massachusetts), Romney need only have consulted Sabelhaus!

Women, Sabelhaus says, are gradually recognizing that money is power, and they are beginning to donate sums that make business and political leaders take notice. "Women are stepping up, commanding attention in their own right. We became change agents because we were willing to write checks, just like the men," she continues. "In the next ten to fifteen years, $130 trillion will roll from one generation to the next, and it will be ours to invest because we live seven years longer than men do. It's a tsunami, and we have to be good stewards for our families and communities. We have to make an impact."

Like Sabelhaus, Jillian Manus has also become a force in both nonprofits and politics. Manus, a bicoastal literary agent and brand-builder with clients like Russell Simmons and Jerry Rice, led the Women's Coalition for Meg Whitman's 2010 campaign for governor, amassing an alliance of more than 100,000 ladies in California. "I linked everyone up, not because they were backing a woman, but because they wanted to get behind the best candidate," she says. "Many people jumped out of their party to back Meg. I had a stealth Democratic coalition, women boldly mobilizing together. We called it 'Megawomen.'"

On behalf of Whitman, who is also her client, and other causes, Manus activates her "Broad Squad," a network aimed at helping women reach their potential and revolutionize society. Manus's Squad has ten rules, including: *We don't whine or judge. We're on call 24-7. You cannot say no to a Squad member. You have to have a philanthropic heart. When you make an ask to the Squad, you have to make sure it's really critical.*

Her nucleus includes fifty-seven women, many of whom are celebrated leaders in their fields and all of whom are 100 percent trustworthy. Manus calls these gals her "No Women" or "Truth Women" because "they'll tell you the hard truths, like your husband is not right for you, or you're not doing the right thing in your job." She estimates that when they multiply their connections and trigger their own Squads, the number of women touched totals more than 11,000.

"Women build a foundation of trust first within these microgroups. From that point on, you are motivated to do whatever you can to help each other," Manus says. "If I want to mobilize or create a movement or visibility for something, I activate the Broad Squad. But it's actually a pyramid of squads, so when I mobilize mine, they mobilize theirs, and then there's a huge rolling thunder."

Sometimes the Broad Squad collaborates to connect professional women, and sometimes members rally to support a candidate. Other times, they work to elevate a neighborhood or to provide comfort in someone's time of need. These women may not all be best girlfriends or even professional colleagues, but together they form a colossus of highly engaged ladies teaming up to make waves.

Manus, who ran Maria Shriver's "Women's Conference" in California from 2003 to 2010 and is a close friend of the former state First Lady, also organized a woman's outreach campaign for former California Governor Arnold Schwarzenegger. Once, when Manus was called at the last minute to appear on *Hardball* with Chris Matthews, she summoned her Squad and the women dropped everything. "Within forty-five minutes I had every policy e-mailed and faxed to me, every position and talking point, every piece of relevant or historical data," she says. "I was armed. I was manned." (Of course, Schwarzenegger was later disgraced by a "women's outreach campaign" all his own, but at the time Manus didn't know his feelers were quite so far-reaching.)

Manus also called upon her Squad one sleepless night when her young son had a 104-degree fever. At 3 AM, she rang a Squad member who is a pediatrician, who within an hour arranged a conference call with other leading doctors around the nation. A tick was found in the boy's ear, and Manus followed instructions to suffocate it with toothpaste to prevent Lyme disease. But she didn't stop there. Because many Squad members do philanthropic work in third-world countries, Manus then wrote a report of the incident to distribute to her ladies, should they ever encounter a similar scourge.

Each year during the holidays, Manus sends her Broad Squad a letter and gift with a theme, such as kindness or peace. "It's intense," she says, "a call to personal action, thinking about what we can do to transform our lives." And all year long, Manus (who sleeps only four hours per night) monitors these women, supporting their ventures and helping behind the scenes. "I work with them to create accountability for each other. I know very few women who don't help other women, and for the handful who don't, it's a big shame on them."

Less JWoww, More Gillibrand

Manus and Sabelhaus aren't the only ones talking politics these days. During election season, women's issues were headline news. Some highlights from the 2012 presidential campaign: Women were excluded from a congressional hearing on birth control. A New York Republican campaign spokesman wrote on his Facebook page, "Let's hurl some acid at those female democratic senators." Rush Limbaugh called a Georgetown student a "prostitute" and a "slut" for wanting access to contraception. Young women deemed "SlutWalks" a nifty way to protest sexual harassment on the nation's campuses. A Senate nominee from Indiana said "God intended" pregnancies resulting from rape. A Senate nominee from Missouri justified his categorically antiabortion stance by claiming that women's bodies somehow block unwanted pregnancies during "legitimate rape." Susan G. Komen for the Cure rescinded funding for Planned Parenthood. The Vatican continued its institution-wide cover-up of pedophile priests, yet blasted assiduous nuns for promoting "radical feminist themes."

Controversies mount almost as fast as the number of American kids raised in poverty—up 41 percent between 2000 and 2010. In this divisive, highly partisan era, many ladies point to Christine

Lagarde of the International Monetary Fund and Germany's Angela Merkel, hanging tough across the pond. Is it too much to ask for a nation with a little less JWoww, a lot more Gillibrand?

There's never been a better moment to dive in, women say. It's time to tackle the hot mess our daughters are inheriting, and it's time to do it together.

"Nobody succeeds here alone. There's a huge shift under way in the nuclear family. People are no longer living lives of top-down, dads in charge," says Mary Hughes, the president of Hughes & Co., a strategic communications and political consulting firm. "What is confounding is that in American culture, the rugged individualist has been the male icon forever. It's been part of our cultural landscape from the get-go. What we're now seeing goes totally against that icon, but I don't think anyone has captured the ascendancy of the female leadership model or style."

Hughes, a Democrat, was the founder and director of the 2012 Project, a national nonpartisan campaign in conjunction with the Center for American Women and Politics at Rutgers University to inspire more women to run for Congress and state legislatures in 2012. She insists this clan mentality existed in politics well before it branched into business.

Back in 1985, Ellen Malcolm founded EMILY's List—an acronym for Early Money Is Like Yeast, that is, it raises dough—to support Barbara Mikulski, who was running for the U.S. Senate in Maryland. Mikulski's advocates realized they had great Rolodexes, so they met in one woman's basement and mailed solicitations. When Mikulski won, the ladies, now empowered, continued to organize on behalf of other women running for office. They helped unearth qualified, pro-choice Democratic female candidates, traveled the country to unite constituents, and pooled their dollars to help these women win. "There are now tens of millions of dollars and hundreds of thousands of supporters who are part of this giving circle," Hughes says. "They're a powerhouse, and at one point they were the largest single funder of Democratic women in history."

And in November 2012, these ladies voted. The Democratic Senatorial Campaign Committee recruited a record number of women candidates, and they placed issues close to women's hearts—from reproductive rights to Medicare—front and center. While some women bristled at pandering, urging their parties to focus on job creation and "speak to us above the waist, not just below," all six Democratic women up for reelection won. Stephanie Schriock, the president of EMILY's List, called Democratic women senators "the first line of defense against the Republican war on women." The 113th Congress now has twenty female senators, the most in U.S. history.

"The phenomenon is not new, but women have finally figured out that what it takes to make us competitive in politics is no different than what it takes to make it in business," Mary Hughes says. "It's maximizing cohesiveness, having both financial and emotional support from people who've been through it. Women find they can do things collectively that we couldn't do alone."

BELIZEAN GROVE:
THE WORLD'S ULTIMATE OLD GIRLS' CLUB

I n Cartagena, Colombia, inside the walls of the old city sits a monastery. Inside the monastery sits a chapel whose high ceilings and heavy gray stone offer protection from the sun. Now, just as 400 years ago, there are no windows, no distractions—just silence. Beyond the chapel are terraces overlooking the sea, where bougainvillea cascades over balconies and warblers sing with wrens. And a courtyard where ladies succumb as their hair curls in the breeze. They lean back in straw chairs, uncross legs beneath lunch tables, smile indulgently at toucans that strut and lunge for bites of their salad and ceviche.

These women, who seldom relax and reflect, have traded business suits for sun hats and flown thousands of miles to commune with friends. They've been told to reveal themselves and learn, engage, and rejuvenate. So that afternoon, they will stroll and shop and talk, and when their feet are sore and their bodies are tired, they will huddle in carriages, lulled by the clip-clop of horse hooves as they make their way through tangled streets. And when a man runs alongside them, strumming his guitar, they will be startled. "Beautiful lady," he will say to a woman who is also a chief executive, "let me sing for you."

Never mind that the monastery is now the Santa Clara Hotel and the chapel was remodeled as a meeting room long ago. In 2011, it was a sanctuary for the Belizean Grove.

Belizean Grove is an under-the-radar constellation of many of the world's most accomplished, powerful women. Drawn from government, banking, technology, and beyond, its members form a rare elite. Each has been tapped, Skull and Bones–style, by an existing member, and each seeks out and grooms new talent. And despite its low profile, Belizean Grove has fast become the ultimate Old Girls' Club.

Yet when Susan Stautberg founded the Grove in 1999, she was just trying to get some friends together. Stautberg had always attended girls' schools, and it felt strange to be surrounded by men in her career. She'd certainly progressed in exciting ways and had been active in female networks, but she wished there were more ways for professional women to really get to know one another. Forming her own group didn't seem so far-fetched. After all, Stautberg had a history of creating what she found missing in the world.

Upon graduating Wheaton College, she'd begun working at Westinghouse/Group W Broadcasting in D.C. Determined to get on air, Stautberg volunteered on weekends to cover any murder, rape, or suicide that came up, all while finishing her master's degree in public and international affairs at night. At age 22, Stautberg set her mind to launching a Washington television bureau. "That's the beauty of youth," she says. "I thought I could do it." But her bosses scoffed; they didn't need a D.C. operation, and even if they agreed, they wouldn't choose some ingenue to run it.

Stautberg focused on getting her own scoops and ingratiated herself with local television stations up and down the East Coast, gaining trust and support for her idea. When she'd convinced enough outposts, she returned to the honchos at Westinghouse, and in 1972, Stautberg became the first woman and one of the youngest people ever to lead a Washington bureau. Far from murders, rapes, and suicides, she now covered the White House and Capitol Hill.

Stautberg was the first television journalist to become a White House Fellow, one of the nation's most prestigious leadership and public service programs, and she worked for both Vice President Nelson Rockefeller and Secretary of State Henry Kissinger, traveling internationally and engaging leaders in both public and private sectors. She concentrated on work and valued her brain over her body, even when male colleagues emphasized different assets. "At various times along the way, whether in the White House and TV bureaus, men would point to the casting couch," Stautberg says. That was one way women could get ahead quickly. "It was very blatant in those days. They'd say, 'You're very attractive and bouncy.' And you'd say, 'Sorry, I'll find another TV station to work for.'"

Stautberg was twenty-nine at the end of the White House Fellows program, when she embarked on her first reinvention. Using the skills she'd acquired in journalism—critical thinking and a yen for information—she launched a career in corporate communications, and at age 32 she married a lawyer for the SEC. When their son, Edward, arrived four years later, Stautberg saw a need to help women navigate new challenges facing her generation.

In those days, she says, women in senior management didn't have kids, and there weren't any guidebooks on how to break the news to bosses, much less manage the transition to motherhood. "I had a geriatric pregnancy. I had my secretary at the hospital, I was dictating notes, and I was on painkillers. You were back in two weeks," she says. "You can't have it all at the same time, but we had to learn that."

Stautberg wrote some of the first books to address the needs of women managing work and families, including *Balancing Acts!: Juggling Love, Work, Family, and Recreation* and *Pregnancy Nine to Five*. "I joked that it should have been called Knocked Up on Top," she deadpans. "That would have been a better title and sold more books."

She released her books through MasterMedia Ltd., a combined publishing house and speakers' bureau she'd founded, where she surfaced the type of material she wanted to read by authors she respected. Stautberg believed women needed to get out front with their ideas, and she would lead by example. She went on *Oprah* to promote her work, but friends soon encouraged her to think bigger. Surely, Stautberg knew about more than just publishing. She was a great connector, constantly learning, exchanging ideas, and matchmaking on a grand professional scale. Why not get paid for doing what came naturally?

Stautberg leveraged her sweeping network to found PartnerCom, a firm that sources chief executives and assembles advisory boards. While directing that operation, building boards composed almost entirely of men, she realized that professional women continued to face significant barriers. And she attacked this dilemma by calling her comrades.

Women began to gather around the dining room table at Stautberg's apartment. They had commenced their careers in the 1970s, but twenty years later, female senior executives were still few and far between. There just weren't a lot of ambitious ladies like them, and they didn't have ways to find each other, much less help one another avoid pitfalls and provide tips for success. Friendship required an important investment of time, and these gals were juggling husbands, children, and demanding jobs that required them to travel. In the struggle to keep up, friends often fell by the wayside. But Stautberg knew these trailblazers had similar issues and experiences, regardless of their professions, and she knew they could learn from and support each other, if only they could find the time.

"I always had a dream to start a Bohemian Grove for women," Stautberg says, referring to one of the nation's most exclusive Old Boys' Clubs. That hush-hush group, an extension of the 140-year-old Bohemian Club in San Francisco, has counted so many rich and powerful men among its ranks—including Presidents Eisenhower, Carter, Nixon, and both Bushes—that it sounds like something from a Dan Brown novel. Indeed, the men of Bohemian Grove, who gather each summer under a canopy of redwoods in Monte Rio, California, are credited with facilitating the Manhattan Project.

"I couldn't afford the redwood forest, but one year I went scuba diving with my son in Belize. I thought, 'This place is far enough out of the way,'" Stautberg continues. "If you made the effort, took three planes and a boat to get there, you were going to bond. You would really get to know people."

> *Ladies invited to Belize had to be trustworthy and respectful, innovative and engaged, curious and passionate, kind and caring, generous and strong. And they had to be fun!*

In 1999, Stautberg called her friend Edie Weiner, the leading futurist, with an idea. Why not get some ladies together and go to Belize? By that time, Stautberg and Weiner had met a number of fascinating females through the International Women's Forum and other organizations of leading businesswomen. Wouldn't it be fun to introduce them?

The two friends decided they couldn't invite just any successful women, and the group ought to be more than an assembly of best buddies. The women had to be compatible and have things in common. Ladies invited to Belize need not have money, but they must have reached high positions in their chosen fields and done it ethically, without stints on the casting couch. They had to be trustworthy and respectful, innovative and engaged, curious and passionate, kind and caring, generous and strong. And, of course, they had to be fun! These women had to be able to laugh at themselves, not take themselves too seriously. Above all, no divas.

Stautberg and Weiner dissected the qualities that made their own friendship so special and set out to replicate them with a wider group. They made a list of friends, and friends of friends, who fit the bill. "It was a lark, nothing major. We just wanted to bring some professional women to meet each other, talk about how to deal with our home lives and careers, how to make the world a better place," Weiner recalls. "It was never intended to shake the world."

Stautberg brought along friends from Washington, like Deborah Wince-Smith, now president and CEO of the Council on Competitiveness, and Marion Blakey, the president and CEO of the Aerospace Industries Association, who before that led the Federal Aviation Administration.

Weiner enlisted her pals, including Marilyn Kawakami, who has been a senior executive at Armani, Ralph Lauren, and Anne Klein, and Debra Duneier, a gemologist and entrepreneur. That inaugural year, twenty-seven women—some of whom had never met, but who trusted Stautberg and Weiner—set off for a remote island off Belize. It was Super Bowl weekend.

We'd Fought So Many Battles

Barbara Colwell, who is now a consultant, says that in 1999, she had no idea what Belizean Grove would become. "I was fifty-four then, on a corporate board, and I never dreamed of the bonding that would take place. That first year was so magical. When I came home, my husband said he never saw me giggle like that."

Colwell's first connection to Stautberg and Weiner was professional. After rising to be the highest-ranking woman at TWA, she went to work for Cigna's property and casualty insurance division. She realized she needed help with consumer marketing and hired Weiner to do some forward-looking industry analysis.

Weiner introduced Colwell to Stautberg at a client meeting, and the women hit it off. And in 1992, when Colwell received a letter from Stautberg announcing the launch of PartnerCom, her advisory board–building business, she thought, "How perfect! Because that's what I needed. Cigna had 60 percent of the energy industry, but I had no idea what was keeping executives in the industry up at night. Susan was able to get a cross-section of really leading people across energy—heads of industry and regulatory people," Colwell says. "That ended up being how I got on my first board of directors. My advisers would go back to their boards and propose me."

Colwell, Weiner, and Stautberg forged a close collaboration. Together, they worked on issues and agendas, hammered out problems, and tried to do their best work. "They made my career in insurance. Ten years later, I knew I would follow Susan and Edie anywhere," Colwell says. "There are certain people who are life-changing, and I put both of them in that category."

So she packed a bag and headed to Belize.

Colwell had a lot of associates in her own industries—insurance and travel—but few outlets to meet people outside. "I was raising kids, and you don't get to know people at a lunch," she says. "But after three planes and a boat to get to Belize, it was like being on that first season of *Survivor*." She knew she would see each woman's true colors.

The group stayed at a down-at-the-heels resort where cottages were so dark that the women couldn't even read. Instead, they gathered around the pool and hot tub to talk. "It was so natural to share issues with work, our parents, being the sandwich generation with divorces and kids," Colwell says. "Being able to have people there know what you mean, talking about mothers and mothers' expectations, what you were or weren't living up to."

Colwell has five sisters, but she found her relationships with these peers in Belize were special in a different way. "My sisters would be bored to tears hearing my stories because they're not in New York, not in similar industries, and I wouldn't have known what to do with their advice," she continues. "This was like other sisters who are professionals. Many of us heard each other's stories and were moved to tears."

Their trials were different from those of most women. One woman admitted to wearing Depends because her company plane had only a men's room, while another described stuffing Kotex in her bra to hide the fact that she was breastfeeding from male colleagues. On a business trip, she was mortified when the plane's cabin pressure caused her to express milk and drenched her shirt. Where else could they talk about things like this?

Their heartache had its own flavor, too. One woman's house had recently caught fire, and while she stood watching all her possessions destroyed, she heard a neighbor comment, "Well, she's never even home"—as though she deserved to lose everything because she was devoted to her career. Other women were going through long, bitter divorces. Most were the only female at high levels at work, and everyone had encountered some form of sexism and discrimination.

Colwell could relate, having experienced similar things herself. As she came close to graduating from Columbia Business School, the instructor prepping students for interviews directed women not to wear wedding rings and to hide the fact that they had children. Later, her first boss at TWA told her, "We have good luck making offers to wives of lawyers because we don't have to pay them so much."

Colwell was grateful for the Women's Movement and benefited from the pressure to hire and promote women in the 1970s. But, she says, once women began moving into senior management, "people didn't know what to do with us." Once, when she emerged from a presentation to the president of TWA, her boss asked what they'd discussed. "He said what he always said: 'Nice suit,'" Colwell recalls. "It wasn't said cruelly. If another woman said it, she'd have meant it. But this president said it because he didn't know what else to say. I think you get inured to it."

Colwell remembers TWA in the 1980s as a coarse, rowdy culture where women dressed like men to fit in. "There were always a lot of inappropriate comments. You had to just pretend you didn't hear them. At least I did, because I wasn't going to change how they felt," she says. "We would just get on with it." She didn't keep pictures of her sons in her office, and she pretended that having children was incidental to her life for fear higher-ups and colleagues would think she wasn't focused. Her husband attended PTA meetings and her boys' school plays since he could duck out of the office without risking the stigma of being distracted by kids. But that caused problems too. "My younger son didn't like it because he said his dad didn't mingle right with the mothers," Colwell says. "He just sat back in the corner and didn't talk."

When twenty-seven women came to Belize with their own tales, their own variations on familiar feelings and predicaments, they found a sympathetic audience. At one point, a senior banker gave one of the most poignant speeches. "She said, 'When I walk into most rooms I know I'm smarter than most of the people there, and I think about whether to keep my mouth closed.' She didn't want anyone to know it," Colwell recalls. "She talked about how out of place she felt as a successful woman, even around other women. A lot of people wouldn't say that, but with this group it resonated. Maybe because we'd fought so many battles."

That first year, women from across industries shared their capabilities and discussed what they were trying to achieve. For many it was a relief to be with other Type A gals who didn't apologize for their ambition and keen intellect. They appreciated those qualities in each other and celebrated their collective success.

"It worked. We talked about some of the grandest global issues as well as the personal things that affected our lives," Weiner says. "We decided, 'Hey, let's do this again next year.'"

A Sisterhood, Not a Business Network

Fourteen years and 150 global members later, Belizean Grove is now much more than a lark. It has gained structure and committees and has evolved to address women's concerns at a new stage of life. The group has picked up some bold-faced names—including Sonia Sotomayor, who resigned from the Grove when she was nominated as a Supreme Court Justice—and still managed to stay anonymous, with members acting as *éminences grises* around the world.

Yet "Grovers" adhere to their initial goal to unite women across disciplines for friendship and learning. "It's an instantaneous group of friends who have been in effect prescreened so they have common characteristics. Many women were the first at what they did, so there's a common experience," says Connie Duckworth, the founder and CEO of ARZU. "We're united in a common set of morals and ethics, a commitment to helping each other and other women."

The women, who are now in their fifties and sixties, may be high achievers, but they insist they are a sisterhood rather than a business network. Many have trouble defining the Grove and often begin by explaining what it's not. It's not a sorority, think tank, leadership organization, engine for innovation, or vehicle for job creation. It's no single one of these things. Rather, it's all of them combined.

Nancye Green, who was CEO of Donovan/Green, a consulting firm, before becoming CEO of Waterworks, says Belizean Grove has always been different from other professional groups. By the time she came to the Grove, in year three or four, she had already been a member of the Young Presidents' Organization for more than a decade. She'd joined YPO when she had a baby daughter, and she remembers its clubby male ethos. Green never felt completely comfortable discussing work/life issues with associates there.

"I was on the board of directors of a well-known U.S. company and got a call from the CEO to discuss an urgent matter. Caitlin had a poopy diaper, but I took the call anyway and I just remember thinking: Guys don't get this part," she says over lunch near her home in Chelsea, in downtown Manhattan. "I remember never feeling in the right place because I always needed to do more for my kids, more for work."

But when Green arrived in Belizean Grove, it felt like coming home. "I very much remember, after having spent fifteen years in YPO, I came back from my first trip to Belize and had never felt so energized in my entire life. It was just intellectual mind candy. Every conversation was deep and interesting," she says. "They got me, what I care about. When you have an issue, they say, 'I get it. Here's my strategy for coping with the same things.'"

Belizean Grove knows no boundaries. Members leave egos and business cards at the door, and their relationships bleed into every area of life. Catherine Allen, who leads the Santa Fe Group consulting firm, recalls that when her fiancé was dying of brain cancer, Grovers opened doors to leading specialists and patient advocates. Then, they supported her as she grieved. "It's hard to make deep friends at this point in your life, but through the Grove we've really made some deep, holistic friendships," she says. "They're people to be in business with, people to travel with. These friendships help you in many ways, both in joy and in sorrow."

> "What happens in the Grove stays in the Grove. If anyone crossed the line, they wouldn't last very long."—Penny Peters

Similarly, when Penny Peters, a marketing and public relations maven, had one of many back surgeries, she couldn't get out of bed. The night she returned from the hospital, another Grover was hosting a cocktail party, and suddenly Peters's phone rang. "Have you eaten yet?" her friends asked. They filled a huge platter of food and arrived at her doorstep, eager to continue the festivities at Peters's bedside. "Trust comes before anything else. People can say anything, talk about troubled children, straying spouses, acknowledge the cancer they haven't told their spouse about while they get the strength to do it," Peters says. "What happens in the Grove stays in the Grove. If anyone crossed the line, they wouldn't last very long."

Still, as any organization grows and matures, some things change. There are personal matters women might reveal before a group of twenty-seven that they won't discuss before 150. But Stautberg and the Grove's membership committee take care to ensure that the heart of the Grove—the bonds that united those initial members—still beats.

Belizean Grove remains by invitation only. One or more Grovers tap potential candidates and escort them through meetings with a membership committee whose vetting process is rigorous. It takes more than a C-suite title to be admitted to Belizean Grove. Applicants need four to six people who can attest to their intelligence, character, and sense of fun. As Stautberg puts it: Brains are good, charm is better, kindness is best. "Everyone has a phenomenal résumé to get into the Grove, but it's not about the résumé. It's an organization about heart, soul, and spirit," she says. "You're talking about your hopes and dreams and ways you want to solve the world's problems. So you don't want someone across the hot tub who's going to judge you. There are lots of VIPs who want to be Grovers, but they're just that—VIPs."

To keep their coterie vibrant and varied, each new member must add to the Grove's overall talents, skills, and diversity. Belizean Grove has corporate titans and artists, lawyers and scientists, academics and nonprofit executives, ambassadors and politicians. They don't need any more Upper East Side investment bankers, but they could use a fire chief, police chief, or union leader. Several years ago, the membership committee sought spiritual guides from an assortment of faiths. And to avoid competition or discomfort, only one employee of any company can be a member of Belizean Grove. "Part of the objective is not to hang with our own industry, but rather to have exposure to a much broader constellation," says Michelle Jordan, a Southern California–based consultant specializing in reputation management and crisis communications. "We encourage diversity so we're able to expose ourselves to new ideas, to meet women from five continents we wouldn't otherwise come across."

Belizean Grove now has a charter and code of conduct and, since its founding in 1999, has had three instances where they've asked someone to leave—situations where members were found to be unethical, had broken trust, or had treated another member disrespectfully. The group accepts no more than twenty newbies each year so it can "on-board," or properly welcome and absorb, each one. New members are assigned "big sisters" who accompany them to meetings and events.

At four-day retreats, which are held in January or February—still on Super Bowl weekend and generally in Central or South America—Grovers introduce themselves at an opening night dinner and are encouraged to mix with participants they don't yet know. Most of the women bunk together, sometimes with strangers so as not to form cliques.

A hallmark of Belizean Grove remains members' insatiable curiosity. Grovers spend mornings in panel discussions based on the retreat's particular theme, which in recent years have included "Complexity," "Shaping Our Future," and "Wisdom and Spirit." Here, members showcase their knowledge, opining on subjects as wide-ranging as military strategy, marine life, philanthropy, and how revolutions in the Middle East will affect the geopolitical balance. While Grovers now invite "global guests," outside speakers who round out the slate, their own members—an assembly of experts—generally populate the dais. Evenings often include a reception at the U.S. embassy with the host country's leading politicians and dignitaries.

"There is a wonderful saying: To be universally interesting, you have to be universally interested," says Stautberg, who weaves meaningful quotes into nearly every casual conversation. "Grove sessions are like catalysts, with people coming from diverse backgrounds and expertise. Ideas bounce off each other and new ideas come out front. We're coming to learn and we want to come back rejuvenated, with a new passion and purpose for what we do."

As Grovers work to better themselves, they also find ways to improve the lives of other women. They've created a younger members' group, the TARAs (Today's Already Rising Achievers), to integrate talented, motivated women in their thirties and forties. And, at an annual auction that raises more than $100,000, Grovers bid on consulting engagements and vacations at members' private homes to sustain the group's "Adventures of the Mind" foundation, which supports women and girls. In every country they visit, Grovers confer with local luminaries to find the most effective nonprofits, and a portion of funds raised is donated to help that nation's women.

"I was always the first woman in anything I did, and I'd seen in my career the number of doors shut if you didn't go along with the casting couch. It would have been nice to have some mentors, so we created a network to make it easier," Stautberg says. "When you see there's a problem out there, you think of ways to solve it. You have to go out and create what you want for yourself and your community. You create a path, but leave markers for others to follow."

Now Stautberg's markers are seen and felt across the globe, as Grovers return from retreats and bring the spirit of sisterhood to their homelands. "I have learned so much from being part of this group—the friendship, network, sorority. Especially for us Latin American women who are basically coming out of our shells right now," says Rosy Del Dago, who joined Belizean Grove in 2010 and helped organize the group's retreat in Colombia. Del Dago, who is leading the construction of a major port in Barranquilla, always worked in her family business under the thumb of a patriarch. Her father only had girls, so he had no choice but to bring them into his company, but Del Dago says she is finally cutting the umbilical cord.

"We didn't venture out, maybe because of insecurity. Our professional projections were very narrow. But as we've continued educating ourselves and being in contact with other women through social activities, it's helped us branch out," she says. "It's been so enriching to meet women around the world who are professionals, who are fun and willing to share their experiences, help each other out. Now I'm venturing out professionally and doing things beyond my family circle."

Del Dago has begun participating in a civic association in Barranquilla and is involved with the Spanish Chamber of Commerce in Miami. Though she's in her mid-fifties and has been on the board of her family business for twenty-five years, Del Dago is just now joining other boards too. She created a foundation to help high-potential Colombian girls in low-income areas, and has begun to gather groups of professional women in Barranquilla once or twice a month. "I got the idea from Belizean Grove and now it's sticking here," she says. "We have one friend who's the first woman mayor of Barranquilla, and we're trying to get women in many different occupations so we have a wide variety of ideas. We invite our friends from Cartagena. It's changed my life, my entire outlook.

"Women here are gaining individuality, relying less on traditional family units," Del Dago continues. "We've had to go out and fend for ourselves, and if we don't find support in the traditional male-oriented organizations, we bond with girlfriends. It helps that our girlfriends are now in positions of power. We lean on each other and grow, and the more strength we have, the more interested we are in making these partnerships. I am not a feminist, but there's strength in our numbers. We have a saying here: *No somos macho, pero somos muchas*. We are not men, but we are many."

Any Way of Being a Girl Is Fine

Tribes need chiefs, and Grovers say Susan Stautberg has always embodied the spirit of Belizean Grove.

Stautberg lives on the seventh floor of a prewar building in Manhattan's Carnegie Hill, a stone's throw from Central Park. Visitors are ushered into a living room that is quiet, stately, and formal, decorated in pale yellow and cornflower blue, the colors of tradition. English horse prints hang above Philadelphia Queen Anne and Chippendale antiques, befitting—as Stautberg is—a descendant of Martha Washington.

Stautberg sits placidly, reflecting on her career and the history of Belizean Grove, and in the background one hears the sound of fingers on keyboards, then a whisper and a laugh. There are women working here. But where?

Past a hallway featuring photos of Stautberg with Gerald Ford, Ronald Reagan, George H. W. Bush, Al Gore—she is proud of her days at the White House—ladies once again convene at Stautberg's table. "Once we had offices in the West Wing, and now we're at the dining room table!" Stautberg smiles at the eager, unlined faces of employees and interns staffed on her various endeavors: the Grove, PartnerCom, and WomenCorporateDirectors (WCD), an association of women on corporate boards that has fifty chapters on six continents, which she founded in this very same room.

A cluster of young ladies in sundresses, two of whom are the daughters of Grovers, squint at laptops; reach for staplers, paper clips, lollipops, and Advil, all strewn across the table; dig into file boxes stacked on the floor; and hop to the fax, printer, or shredder, stationed a few feet away. From under a bell jar, a small, rare weather vane of Miss Liberty, with some of its original gilt still intact, watches over the group. "Mother collects antiques and always had it on her farm in Pennsylvania. She gave it to me a few years ago," Stautberg says. "It's always an inspiration to me."

The other end of the long table is set formally for lunch. When the women are ready to break from e-mailing CEOs, drafting speeches, and organizing events, they will take silver in hand, place cloth napkins in laps, and eat sandwiches on Stautberg's fine china. They might look up to admire sterling candlesticks and bowls of flowers before them. In all the years Stautberg worked in the White House or at 9 West 57th Street, she never thought she'd wind up based at home. But it works.

> *Inside Stautberg and her Grovers lives a juxtaposition: that of public and private, professional and personal, stolid and vulnerable, serious and silly. Philadelphia Queen Anne and Chippendale coexist with hot pink and turquoise.*

Travel further into Stautberg's inner sanctum, past the kitchen with its map of the world, under the flag of Belizean Grove, and into her control rooms. Brace for a blast of color. Back here, where guests would never venture uninvited, Stautberg has transformed maids' rooms into offices that explode with memorabilia from Belizean Grove adventures: vivid tapestries and devilish masks, flamingoes and painted suns, fish fashioned from coconut shells, a framed wine-stained cocktail napkin. There's the famous bell Stautberg uses to quiet Grovers, "which is like herding elephants with a toothbrush." And a photo of Edie Weiner in a spiky wig, singing with the Shirelles at Stautberg's sixtieth birthday party.

Bookshelves are spilling over. There's a photograph from the redwood forest with a sign pointing to Bohemian Grove. A card picturing two old broads with saggy boobs, pink hair, and martini glasses is displayed beside a note from Sonia Sotomayor. The whole suite is painted hot pink and turquoise.

At first it's a shock, as if two siblings—the straight arrow and the black sheep—still occupy the same turf. How could these rooms, with their muddle and whimsy, belong to a blueblood Colonial Dame? Yet maybe that's the point. Inside Stautberg and her Grovers lives a juxtaposition: that of public and private, professional and personal, stolid and vulnerable, serious and silly. Philadelphia Queen Anne and Chippendale coexist with hot pink and turquoise.

"That's the essence. We meet very successful women every day and there's one face on them. But it's seeing beyond that public facade and allowing her to be a whole person, to show her hot pink and turquoise. When you put both parts together, you get an incredible explosion," says Theresa Behrendt, who befriended Stautberg thirty years ago in Washington, D.C., and is now a political fundraiser and co-owner of a horse-racing enterprise. "The creativity, the partnerships, people who have formed businesses, written books, introduced each other to husbands. This is all Susan Stautberg."

Many Grovers see the open, accepting nature of their sisterhood encapsulated in the unique friendship of Stautberg and Weiner, whose backgrounds could not be more different. Some say they represent yin and yang, serving as a magnetic force to draw diverse women together.

Weiner grew up poor in New York and was sent to live in foster homes when her mother, who had multiple sclerosis, could no longer care for her three children. "Edie talks about having everything she had in a box, ready to go to the next foster home. It was so hard that she didn't have a mother," Barbara Colwell says of her life-changing friend. "Edie is all heart with no hang-ups about class or anything. She's brilliant, honored all over the world, and just cares if you're a good person."

Stautberg, meanwhile, went to prestigious prep schools and belongs to tony clubs in Manhattan and Newport, Rhode Island, where her family owned The Elms, one of the historic mansions on Bellevue Avenue. But an upper-crust upbringing never stifled her sense of humor. Every summer weekend at her elite beach association, Stautberg joins a dozen friends for water aerobics and, to combat the boredom of treading water, each must arrive with a new bawdy joke. Weeks in advance, Stautberg finds herself trolling the Internet for quips, and by Labor Day she's filed away enough wisecracks to last her all year. Just as with her beloved quotes, she delights in disrupting amiable chitchat with a zinger. Stautberg isn't one to go to the barricades; she'd no sooner burn a bra than a book. Hers is a quiet subversion, and she agitates from inside the establishment.

> In Belizean Grove, women babble in nonlinear ways, delighting in tangents that would get them booed out of Harvard Business School.

"Susan is a Republican. She looks like the most corporate or political person, but she takes all sorts of risks. She herself is such a combination of business and pleasure and fun. And Edie is an Independent who often leans Democrat. She's wild, outspoken, out there," Nancye Green says. "The group is filled with color and texture. In the Grove, any way of being a girl is fine."

So Belizean Grove moves, in character and practice, in concentric circles outward from Stautberg and Weiner. It embraces members from every religion, race, socioeconomic background, and political persuasion, from Communist to Tea Party. The ladies pride themselves on being a model of civility. "You can sit any two of these women down outside the Grove and they would disregard each other because they're on opposite ends of the political spectrum," Weiner says. "But when they're at the Grove, they're thinking about how can we help each other achieve, or how can I help share what I know to make life easier or better for you."

In Belizean Grove, women babble in nonlinear ways, delighting in tangents that would get them booed out of HBS. In one breath, they're discussing the influences of nanotechnology, and in the next they're talking about where to get their nails done. "We can go back and forth from business to personal. In a paragraph we can do four different topics. It's 'I love your necklace,' then we move on to careers," Stautberg says. "It's 'I have this problem. How are we going to solve it?' We try to be brave about whatever it is."

Speaking of necklaces, Stautberg often wears elastic bands of bright beads—hot pink, yellow, turquoise, and green orbs, each painted with a cocktail glass, the sun and moon, an airplane, flip-flops, palm trees, and shells. All symbols of Grovers at rest. "Men have their ties, and we have our jewelry. You can see another Grover and know it." Stautberg's eyes soften and she grins mischievously. Jewelry isn't the only frivolity embraced by these women who, because of their public positions, have to be buttoned up most of the time. For Belizean Grovers, excitement doesn't mean noisome cavorting—the widespread drunkenness, peeing on redwoods, and dressing in drag reputedly favored by their Bohemian counterparts. The ladies prefer emotional bonding to bacchanal. But that doesn't mean they can't have a little fun, and the Grove is their place to let loose.

Since the night members wore wigs to startle the U.S. ambassador to Belize, hairpieces and flamboyant hats have played a starring role at retreats. Reverend Sylvia Sumter, the senior minister at Unity of Washington, D.C., church, recalls donning a big blond wig and hand-me-down bustier while delivering a spiritual talk at her first Grove weekend. "There's a tradition passed down when you're new. At the end of my talk, I got to pick the newbie who would wear it the next year," she laughs. "These things are necessary. We're showing a willingness to be vulnerable, exposed, honest, and authentic—in addition to the talents and wisdom and skills everyone brings."

Prominent women in wigs and bustiers is, well, goofy. But that's the idea: to access all parts of their personalities, especially the light and silly ones kept under wraps in their high-powered lives. Weiner likens it to seeing a politician you admire at a roast or costume party. You realize she is more than a public persona. She is a human being.

"There are things we do that help us say, 'Hey, this world is bigger than all of us.' We laugh and don't take ourselves so seriously. We can point to each other and say, 'I love you, you're nuts,' and that helps form this deep commitment, a feeling of 'I would lie down in front of a bus for you. Prove to me you don't think you're queen of the world and I will be there for you,'" Weiner says. "When you take a diamond, you can't focus on any one facet. No two women or diamonds are alike. We try to create a program once a year for us to get to know each other before we're scattered to the wind, to hit on all the facets of these diamonds."

Many portray Grove retreats as lifetimes, with a full range of emotions, compressed into weekends. There are times to celebrate and times when people cry. Together, Grovers dance like no one's watching.

I Got–You Got

Bohemian Grove's motto, "Weaving Spiders Come Not Here," which advises members against actively promoting themselves and pursuing business, applies to Belizeans as well. Belizean Grove is not meant to be commercial or transactional, but if it all sounds a bit "kumbaya," think again.

Grovers form a power base. They serve on the boards of companies like Goldman Sachs Bank USA, NASDAQ, Nordstrom, DSW, PetSmart, and REI. Members also include movie producers, a Canadian senator, a presidential candidate in Peru, and the former COO of the Episcopal Church. These gals are in positions to make things happen.

Inevitably, because business is such a big part of their lives, work is discussed and plans are conceived. In the early days, Stautberg encouraged Grovers to stand at retreats and voice their asks and offers, what she calls *I got–You got's*. Women would request what they needed—be it help with their careers, buying tables at a charity event, a nanny or summer internship for their kids, or a date with a fabulous man—and put forth what they might share with others. As the Grove expanded, *I got–You got's* migrated to the newsletter, but members say this exchange of favors happens organically all the time, as women share news of their undertakings.

The ladies have written books together, formed companies together, invested together, and helped members break into that final bastion of male rule, the corporate board. They've also mentored and hired each other's kids. There are hundreds, if not thousands, of examples of Grovers opening Rolodexes and wallets on each other's behalf. Grovers can't always connect the dots or point to one person who provided the necessary rocket fuel to succeed. They don't promote themselves, but their projects seem to come together. They hang out, they mention things, and wheels are set in motion. "There's something about female energy—feeling like you're planting seeds all the time. Your value is connected to the value you create, whether with children, people who work for you, whom you mentor," Nancye Green says. "Once we've helped each other, it's intensely satisfying."

Grovers also guide each other through periods of transition. Pernille Spiers-Lopez, who left Ikea in 2011 after twenty-one years, says the Grove gave her the courage to branch out. "I don't think I would have made this decision if I didn't have a network of people to work this through with. The Grove helps you ask the questions, dare to do something different. And if you do, you know you're not alone," she says. "I'm not walking off a steep cliff. I'm taking a break, and there will be support along the way. I have no fear because of this network of people behind me."

Spiers-Lopez believes many people would love to change their lives and livelihoods, but stop short because they're afraid. They are plagued by existential doubts: Will I still be relevant? Will I be forgotten? Who am I without a title? As opposed to other professional networks, Belizean Grove doesn't equate members' worth with their occupations.

"Other business networks see people as the job they hold and how useful they are to you. The great heart and strength of the Grove is that it's full of people who've made and are continuing to make great achievements, but it's not commercial or transactional. There's a broader, richer value system," says Jane Diplock, who chaired both the executive committee of the International Organization of Securities Commissions and the New Zealand Securities Commission, and who sits on the board of the Singapore stock exchange. "If you don't know what the Grove can offer, you don't miss it. You don't realize these enormously beneficial relationships get people to take charge of their destinies, which is different from getting the next job on the ladder."

Here Come the Women

Penny Peters has a summer birthday, but her Grover friends began calling in March. They needed to pin down dates when she would be available for a party. It was, after all, her sixty-fifth.

In June, Peters planned to be in Beijing with Barbara Colwell for a WomenCorporateDirectors event, and then she would race to New Mexico for the Santa Fe International Folk Art Market with another group of Grovers. Peters had neither time nor energy for fanfare, but her pals insisted on a party and she reluctantly agreed. Then she promptly forgot.

When Peters returned from China, she was surprised by voice mails and e-mails from Grovers saying, "See you Tuesday."

Tuesday turned out to be an assault of New York summer—hot, humid, raining on and off—but the Grovers decided to meet outdoors anyway. Peters was due in Central Park at 6 PM, but she was jet-lagged and late and couldn't find the pants she wanted to wear. She still hadn't unpacked from her trip. She looked for wine, or anything she could contribute to the festivities, but her cabinets were bare after weeks away. She grabbed some candles and walked out the door.

As Peters followed the path from West 81st Street, clouds began to lift and part, and the sun came out. Suddenly it was bright, and when she caught sight of her friends, she gasped. There, on a spit of land stretching into a pond encircled by tall grasses, the women had laid a patchwork of colorful blankets. Along the perimeter they'd placed makeshift tables, cardboard boxes covered with red, yellow, and blue plastic cloths. There were hors d'oeuvres, cheeses, salads, vegetables, pastas, chicken, and ribs, not to mention turkey meatloaf sandwiches from a Grover's husband's secret recipe and a homemade three-tiered cake. To Peters, it looked like a 1970s potluck wedding banquet. Everyone had brought something special.

> This is the true spirit of Belizean Grove: women who have been business partners and dearest friends, who take pride and great joy in teaming up to improve lives and communities, who use their collective power for good.

Peters has been collecting shawls since she was twenty years old, so as a tribute guests were told to wear some sort of wrap. Since it was hot, they'd decided instead to drape and weave the fabric through branches of surrounding trees. When Peters lifted her gaze, she saw ribbons of pink, red, orange, yellow, green, blue, and gold.

She descended into a field of family and friends, abuzz in the shadow of Belvedere Castle. But before Peters could even put down her bag, she was engulfed by a gaggle of giddy ladies. When they finally dispersed, she was wearing hot pink zebra sunglasses, a pink and purple sparkly tiara, and a purple feather boa—an ensemble she sported all night. She directed her fifty guests with a glow-in-the-dark magic wand.

It was the summer solstice, the longest day of the year, but fireflies were already emerging. Lights from the Delacorte Theater twinkled on the horizon, a reminder of Peters's lifelong love of the stage. It felt like a scene from *A Midsummer Night's Dream*.

This, Peters says, is the true spirit of Belizean Grove: women who have been business partners and dearest friends, who take pride and great joy in teaming up to improve lives and communities, who use their collective power for good. These women are like sisters, their bonds like blood ties. She knows they will see her through the rest of her days.

Peters was raised in the classic Jewish tradition and taught to repair the world. Men do it independently, while women do it in packs. So, she wonders, what happens when these coffee klatches and quilting bees are unleashed on the globe and given a new platform? What happens when women bring this caring, collaborative spirit into business? What ensues when the sisterhood infuses the workplace, when Grove-like connections multiply?

"It's not just about what women will achieve for themselves. It's adding women to the mix *with* men. It's about having two styles of problem solving simultaneously. It may help us win back a place for our country. It means we'll have better promise for our children, greater social welfare and understanding, a healthier planet and environment, *and* economic success," Peters says. "Because we've been functioning on half a brain. Men have been doing a fine job, but they've just been doing half. . . .

"Here come the women."

CONCLUSION:
CREATING YOUR OWN
STILETTO NETWORK

S tiletto Networks are already changing the world. A movement has begun, but the purpose of this book is not just to identify it. It's to catalyze it as well. Why shouldn't more women back each other like the Indians of TiE? Why shouldn't they be angling to make their companies and schools and communities and cities and countries better for themselves and others? Why shouldn't they be banding together and tipping the scales?

Each Stiletto Network is as unique as the women it convenes, but they do have common characteristics. Their stories provide lessons and tips to help others forge their own groups.

• **Start now (the younger the better)!** It doesn't matter if you're a public company CEO, an entrepreneur, a middle manager, a freelancer, a stay-at-home mom, or a college student. You don't need to be famous or fabulous to create a Stiletto Network, and you need not begin with major connections. In fact, the earlier women get started, the tighter and stronger their groups become. Just as Kathi Lutton said (in Chapter 5), college students can create networks overnight by assembling friends and organizing events for accomplished female alumnae. And, as Mallun Yen (Chapter 2) and Sukhinder Singh Cassidy (Chapter 5) described, when women unite early in their careers, they're more likely to steer each other toward promotions and opportunities, counsel each other through difficulties, and ultimately become powerful—together.

• **Think diversity.** Stiletto Networks aren't cabals of best buddies. In fact, they shouldn't be. And they can't be simply stocked with employees from the same firm. While there's no singular formula, the most effective groups draw women with diverse skills from across a variety of industries. They introduce women who might not otherwise meet. They keep members' thinking fresh, expand their horizons, and increase their spheres of influence.

• **Filter for relevance and shared experience.** Still, for Stiletto Networks to gel, women should have some shared traits. For instance, The Vault, 4C2B, Babes in Boyland, and Lady Business each connect women from different industries, but members of each group are about the same age or level of expertise. Similar experiences and touch points allow women to quickly build the bonds of trust and loyalty at the heart of these networks.

• **Believe in the magic.** Stiletto Networks don't need a specific goal or agenda at the onset, and as Gerry Laybourne said (Chapter 8), they shouldn't try to "right the wrongs of oppression." They need only bring together women with shared values and ethics, women who are open to aiding others. If you get dynamic ladies talking or walking or drinking, exciting things will happen.

• **Strike a balance between personal and professional.** We've all been to book groups where ladies drink wine, chat about friends and family, and then . . . Oops! Time's up and no one's discussed the book. And we've all been to networking events where humanity is lost, where we feel surrounded by cardboard cutouts. Stiletto Networks must be purposeful, yet not feel like another work function. They must address the needs of women present, yet still retain the fun. One way to do this is to appoint a different woman to lead each meeting, or like The Vault, to feature guest speakers and establish discussion topics in advance.

• **Have courage, give courage.** Stiletto Networks push members to pursue their passions and take risks. Members should help each woman script difficult conversations (e.g., about promotion or compensation), and shouldn't be afraid to disagree. Just like Gerry Laybourne was grateful when Maggie Wilderotter "walked [her] to the woodshed" (Chapter 8), and just as Jillian Manus said of her Broad Squad (Chapter 10), we all need friends who tell us hard truths. Speak up when members of your Stiletto Network are making bad decisions or undermining themselves, but do it with kindness.

• **Raise profiles.** 2012 may have been "The Year of the Woman," but according to the 4th Estate, a project run by the media monitoring service Global News Intelligence, women were notably underrepresented in coverage of the 2012 presidential election, generally comprising less than 20 percent of sources quoted in the mainstream media. Stiletto Networks can change those statistics. These groups spur women to become visible leaders through a conscious commitment to raising profiles and making their voices heard. They should ensure that each woman establishes herself as an expert, lands speaking engagements, and gets media coverage for her endeavors.

• **Use technology to facilitate.** Continue the conversation after you've left dinner and gone back to your offices. Keep thinking and communicating. Make it a regular habit to e-mail articles or data that could be of interest to your coterie. Create private LinkedIn groups to further discussion, follow each other and retweet posts on Twitter, and Like and Share each other's Facebook comments. This idea exchange should become part of everyday life.

• **Systematize "asks and offers."** Women have trouble asking for help. They don't want to appear weak or step on toes. Many groups—like Belizean Grove, Carole Hyatt's Leadership Forum, and now the "Alley to the Valley" series of conferences—have discovered that making "asks and offers" part of a standard process helps members overcome their fear or hesitation. But members should always try to give more than they take.

• **If possible, go away together.** As Barbara Colwell, the Belizean Grover, said, women don't really get to know each other at lunch. It's hard to foster real and true relationships when pulled in many directions. Some of the most cohesive Stiletto Networks—like Belizean Grove or Silvia Fernandez's venture capital gals—plan an annual getaway. There, members relax and let loose, solidifying and deepening friendships.

• **Play with boys!** It's nice to be pro-women, and it's great to help advance qualified girlfriends. But no one works in a vacuum. The best way to change "the comfort formula" is by making introductions and investments with guys too. So think about how to build personal and political capital with men, and incorporate them into your lives and ventures. Integration, not isolation, is the goal.

INDEX